Panic to

Profits

Be Your Own

Best Prophet

One Breath at a Time

by

Terry Anne Wohl

© 2011 Terry Anne Wohl

C.P. Certified Practitioner,

LMT, NCTMB, Member of AOBTA

Certified Mind-Body-Vibrancy Coach, D.D. Doctor of Divinity

All rights reserved. No part of this book may be reproduced or transmitted in any form or by any means without the prior written permission of the author.

Based on the

B.E.S.T. Course

B	-	Believe in Yourself
E	-	Embrace Emotional Management Skills
S	-	Support That Works for You
T	-	Trust Your True Voice and Purpose

By Terry Anne Wohl

Acknowledgments

It is through the grace of God and the compassionate support of my circle of family, friends, and professional associates that I am able to bring you this book. I would like to acknowledge and thank my family and friends for their ongoing love, loyalty, and encouragement. They have motivated me to work through my challenges and embrace a life of balance, productivity, leadership, and well-being.

Marion Dickes, the President of the World Healing Ministry was also one of my motivating spiritual guides. To this day, her loving words are still posted on the border of my computer. In one of her many letters to me, she wrote, *"Dear Terry, You are the only you in the whole world and universe, and you do know what you are meant to do – to express and fulfill the divine idea in you before you incarnated. It is a sacred and precious trust to keep. . . . Write your book. . . . Assure yourself that as you establish and pursue your path, God will sustain and support you because it is God's Work. . . . Love yourself more than ever before. Love, Marion."*

There have been so many wonderful teachers, mentors, and support systems in my life. Included in this long list are: Ethel Lombardi, Margot Anand, Ohashi, Gay and Katie Hendricks, Kam Yuen, Fred Shafer, Jamie Smart, Vrinda Norman, Jerome Lazar, Bob Burnham, Marty Couch, Lisa Sassevich, Jenn August, Arleen Prairie, Jay Hand, Reverend Erica, members of Unity in Chicago, MaryAine Curtis, Maya Hersioux, Robert Blau, and Stephanie Chambers.

Dedication

This book is dedicated to all people who are willing to evolve their spirits, souls, hearts and bodies by continuing to learn and grow from all of their experiences in life.

May you choose the thoughts and feelings of remembrance that you are Divine Perfection just as you are!!!!

Remember that you can embrace your goodness and awareness of Your Divine Presence by choosing to be in charge of your empowering thoughts,
one breath at a time.

Akashic Record and Channeling Prayer

Divine Essence,

Love ever Present Grace Embracing All,

I call forth:

The Divine Feminine

The Divine Masculine

The Highest Beings of Light,

The Archangels,

Keepers of the Akashic Records,

Masters, Guides,

The Highest Frequencies of our Loved Ones, and Mentors.

I call forth our opening awareness and reception of the highest and most nourishing vibrations and information for the greatest Well-being at this time.

In Grace, I give thanks for making me a Clear Channel for the well-being of ALL.

Beverly Brunelle and Terry Wohl created this prayer to help you access the Akashic Records, so that you may transcribe the messages you receive in your meditations. A similar prayer was utilized the author bring forth much of the information included in this book.

Table of Contents

Panic to 1
Profits 1
Be Your Own 1
Best Prophet 1
One Breath at a Time 1
by 1
Terry Anne Wohl 1
    Acknowledgments 3
    Dedication 4
    Akashic Record and Channeling Prayer 5
    Table of Contents 6
    Introduction 10
        Origin of the Book 11
        How to Use this Book 12
        Summary of the Sections 13
Part One: Beliefs, Emotions, and Transformation 17
    Chapter One: Stress Management 18
        1. Stress Management Techniques 18
        2. Deep Breathing 19
        3. Enhance Your Listening Skills 24
        4. Manage Your Stress States to Become More Resourceful 33

    5. Homework Exercises 45
Chapter Two: Empower Your Beliefs................................ 48
    1. Introduction 48
    2. Definitions of Beliefs 50
    3. Key Components of Beliefs 52
    4. Key Points About Beliefs.. 56
    5. Factors Affecting The Formation Of Beliefs 63
    6. Identity Beliefs 67
    7. Hidden Beliefs 70
    8. Reframing the Situation to Create More
       Empowering Beliefs... 72
    9. Beliefs about Happiness... 82
    10. PV to BV, Symbols and Beliefs. 85
    11. Beliefs, Jesus, and Healing 86
    12. Exercises 87
Chapter Three: Enlightenment about Emotions 90
    1. Introduction 90
    2. Sex and Emotions 91
    3. Feelings and Emotions 96
    4. The Physiology of Emotions.................................... 97
    5. Touch and Emotions... 100
    6. Emotional Literacy 101
Chapter Four: All about Transformation...................... 104
    1. The B.E.S.T. System 105
    2. Transformation Defined 107
    3. The Power of Dissatisfaction!................................ 107

    4. Steps to Transformation 109

    5. Five Element Theory; Creation Cycle 110

    6. Identity Transformations 112

    7. Connecting Your Subconscious and Conscious Minds 122

    8. The "Trance" and "Trans" in "Transformation". 125

    9. Spells and the Subconscious 127

    10. Reverse Engineering 128

    11. Homework to Create the Transformation You Desire 130

Part Two: Additional Resources 132

  Chapter Five: Drama Triangles and Relationships ... 133

    1. The Three Positions 135

    2. Getting Off the Drama Triangle 141

  Chapter Six: Recapitulation for Transformation 163

    1. Recapitulation 163

    2. Reclaiming Lost Parts of Your Soul 165

  Chapter Seven: Trinities of Manifestation 168

    1. Thoughts, Feelings and Actions 169

    2. Ethereal, External and Internal Teams 169

  Chapter Eight: Putting It All Together 171

    1. Stress Management 171

    2. Emotional Literacy 171

    3. Working with Your Subconscious Mind 172

    4. Transforming Beliefs 173

    5. Support Systems 173

6. An Evolutionary Journey versus a Final Destination 174
7. Physical Activity 174
8. 21 Days (or fewer) to Reinforce New Habits 175
9. Continuing Your Progress 175
10. A Blessing for Your Journey 178

Works Cited 180

Internet Sites 183

About the Author 186

Introduction

Why I titled this book: "Panic to Profits, Be Your Own Best Prophet, One Breath at a Time"

This title is directly related to some of the most astounding results experienced by the students who have attended my courses and applied the course-related techniques to their lives. Most of us have been taught to look for answers and solutions that originate from other people. However, in my own life and work, when I began consciously utilizing the mantra: *"If it is meant to be, it is up to me,"* I began to experience tangible results both in my own life and the lives of my students and clients. This book gives you powerful tools to create more abundance in your life and develop more trust in your own guidance and internal resources.

The material of this book is also related to my forty-plus year search for the best ways to heal the shame, blame, anger, and pain that I experienced for the first several decades of my life. Read this book with an open heart and mind. Then take what you have received in this book, think about it, try the suggested exercises on for size, and then keep what works for you and let the rest go.

You may find that you return to this book at a later time and find things in it that you missed the first time around! If you know someone who can benefit from the information, stories, and processes shared in this book, you can order a copy from my website: *www.terrywohl.com*.

Origin of the Book

Much of the material in this book is based on the six-week B.E.S.T. course (previously called "B.E.E.") that I taught at Unity in Chicago in the spring of 2010. However, all the names of the participants have been changed. During this course, several of the participants experienced extraordinary results. A few are listed below:

- A 50% reduction in blood pressure medication – as a result of practicing the stress-reducing techniques in this book
- Acquiring a great six month part time $70,000 management job to avoid bankruptcy
- A reduction in depression symptoms
- Healing from a broken heart and failed relationship
- Recovery from the shame-based relationships and situations
- Clearer communication skills with co-workers
- A deeper sense of peace and well-being
- Increased income and cash flow
- Better health
- Greater sense of contentment

Do you think that these results sound too good to be true? It is impossible to predict the outcome of your own personal experience; however, the results listed above did happen to the participants who were open to the techniques and concepts offered through my teachings.

It is my hope and intention that this book will be one of the significant steps in your evolutionary process as well.

How to Use this Book

This book presents concepts that I offer my course participants in my coaching and bodywork sessions. In the following chapters, I will share these concepts, the principles behind them, and ways to incorporate them into everyday life. The responses of my students and clients to these concepts, their stories, and my own personal stories help make this body of work come alive.

I recommend that you read through the entire book and then pick a particular chapter that piques your interest. Try out the exercises included in the chapter. You may want to pick a buddy who will help you practice these concepts.

By the time you reach the final page of this book, it is my intention that you will have:

- Found processes that work for you.

- Gained tools to decrease your stress and increase your ability to relax.

- Understood the paradox of relaxation and renewal to feel more alive.

- Expanded your presence on this earth plane.

- Found a way to express your true talents.

- Set up a plan and strategy to help you fulfill your life's dreams.

- Experienced greater vitality and well-being.

- Opened up to a greater sense of resourcefulness.

- Acquired a greater sense of grace and well-being.

Create a Clear Outcome

Set your number one priority, then use stress management techniques to help you maintain your focus and motivation.

When you purchase a ticket to travel to a particular destination, what images, sensations, and emotions motivate you to find a way to reach your destination? This principle is also true for all transformational work. It is not as important to know what you don't want as it is to know what you do want! Why? Because at any one time you are focusing on either where you are and don't want to be or on where you want to be. If you keep your focus on where you don't want to be, it will be very difficult to find your way to your true goal.

This book and accompanying course will help you keep your focus on what will give you the most benefit and power to move forward with your life.

Get ready to be positively transformed in the areas of your life where you most desire to be transformed!

Summary of the Sections

Part 1. Beliefs, Emotions, and Transformation

In the first section of this book we will explore the foundations of transformation. Understanding the origins of conscious and unconscious beliefs from creation to transformation will enable you to achieve the changes you desire to create in your life.

Belief work needs to be coupled with the development of your emotional skills. This can be achieved by developing new ways to understand and harness your emotions.

These emotions can also be the key to accessing your subconscious mind to create the powerful changes you desire to experience in your internal and external worlds.

Chapter One: Stress Management. Here are you able to gain easy keys to put into practice immediately. These keys involve increasing your awareness skills, deepening your breathing, setting effective goals, and transforming your internal dialogue. This chapter includes stories and responses of students. You will find easy to do exercises at the end of the chapter.

Chapter Two: Empower Your Beliefs. In this chapter, we cover ways to understand the nature of beliefs and how to create and implement beliefs that help you experience more of what you want in life and less of what you don't want. We also explore the ways in which leaders have helped people address their limiting beliefs, as well as how they have given them the tools to express empowered thoughts and actions.

Chapter Three: Enlightenment about Emotions. Here we examine ways to understand, heal, accept, and maximize the power of your emotions. Consider the way an artist utilizes colors. The artist is able to see the variations of each color. For instance, the painter does not just see green, he is aware of many shades of green, such as Viridian Green, Phthalo Green, Chrome Oxide Green, Sap Green, and Permanent Green Light. This needs to be true of understanding emotions because there are so many subtitles to emotions. Rather than just realizing that you are feeling anger, sadness, fear, and joy, it is possible to understand the various shades of these feelings. This understanding will help you make the best choices in interpreting and utilizing these emotions to motivate you to be pro-active. Thus you will learn to be more masterful with the understanding and management of your emotions.

Chapter Four: All About Transformation. In this chapter, we explore the issues involved in understanding the process of transformation, as well as helpful techniques to achieve the results you desire. Some of the topics we cover are: a system you can use to achieve your transformation, ways to connect with your subconscious mind to reset your internal system, and homework to carry through with your commitment to transform your life in a way that helps you to experience LESS of what you don't want and MORE of what you do!

Part 2. Additional Resources:

Some people are able to just take the information described above and apply it directly to their lives. However, if you are like most people and would benefit from support systems and additional tools and concepts to accelerate the process, then you find these chapters to be as helpful as the preceding ones.

Chapter Five: The Drama Triangle Transforming Relationships. In this chapter we explore the various positions of the Drama Triangle, learn the dynamics of each position, and most importantly learn the best ways to disentangle from Drama Triangle based relationships.

Chapter Six: The Power of Recapitulation. In this chapter, you learn an ancient shamanic technique that will help you retrieve your core energy and let go of the energy distortions that you may have unintentionally picked up from other people, animals, places and things.

Chapter Seven: Trinities of Manifestation. In this chapter, you become aware of the trinity of thoughts, feelings and actions. And you also learn about the Manifestation Trinity of ethereal, external and internal teams.

Chapter Seven: Putting It All Together: Making Transformation Last! In this chapter, we look at various ways to integrate the concepts presented in this book. An essential aspect of maintaining your transformation is the support system you create to sustain the new, improved you.

Part One:

Beliefs, Emotions, and Transformation

Chapter One: Stress Management

1. Stress Management Techniques

In the past twenty years of teaching students from all walks of life, I noticed that no one is immune to stress. In fact, when I recently taught two groups of students at a local college of oriental medicine, the biggest complaint the students expressed was the amount of stress they were feeling in their present lives.

Is this true for you, as well? Do you find that sometimes it is difficult to concentrate and sometimes it is challenging to keep up with all of your daily demands, as well as to get a good night's sleep?

If so, then this is the place for you to start in this book. In this chapter we cover empowering techniques to create a greater sense of relaxation, alertness, and ease in your life. We accomplish this by learning the benefits of and techniques to:

1. Breathe deeply

2. Be aware of your current emotional states (*Chapter Three*)

3. Increase your listening skills

4. Strengthen your central nervous system

5. Utilize the four keys to stress management that were developed by neuroscientists to improve

performance and increase the sense of resourcefulness of the U.S. Navy Seals. These four keys are:

A. Goal setting

B. Mental Rehearsal

C. Self-Talk

D. Arousal Control.

As you can see from this list, I am not reinventing the wheel, so to speak. Instead, I am creating a synthesis of the most effective ways that I have personally experienced to help me and other people live the best lives possible.

2. Deep Breathing

According to *The Heart of Yoga,* by T.K.V. Desikachar, **"The breath is the intelligence of the body."** (Desikachar, p. 22). There are many yogic and healing practices that focus on helping a person learn to breathe deeply. Deep breathing can help a person reduce stress, release endorphins, and stop the internal endless cycles of negative self-talk.

When a client first lies down on my Shiatsu/Thai massage mat, I request that he or she focus on breathing deeply. To help the client feel more comfortable with my request, I often quote Michael Gach (founder of the Acupressure Institute in San Francisco), *"Most people are members of the shallow breathing club."* Just mentioning this idea to clients dissipates some of their self-consciousness and tension. Sometimes clients will say that their minds get in their way and keep them from relaxing. Rather than criticize clients for over-thinking the situation, I acknowledge the strength of their minds and ask them to think of their minds as an ally. If they are willing to harness their minds to notice when they are drifting back into shallow breathing, they can then choose to breathe deeply again.

In fight/ flight/ and freeze conditions, the breath becomes shallow and constricted. This shallow breathing is an autonomic response designed to assist the person to go into a state of hyper-alertness. When a person is faced with a traumatic situation, there is a strong probability that the person will move into an altered trance-like state. A person in this state is more susceptible to negative programming. Whatever is said in these altered-state moments of mental and emotional consciousness takes root in the unconscious mind. Have you ever noticed that whatever was said to you in the middle of a fight tends to come back and haunt you in the form of negative self-talk? *One of the most effective ways to break this perpetual pattern of negative self-talk involves shifting the breath to deep-belly breathing.* This one shift changes the physiological state of the person and releases him or her from the place of negative self-talk accompanied by shallow breathing.

Peter A. Levine states, "Trauma is about the loss of connection to ourselves, to our bodies, to our families, to others in the world around us" (Levine, *Healing Trauma*, p. 9). By making a simple shift of breathing deeply, one is able to re-establish a connection to one's body and establish a greater sense of ease and relaxation.

I told the following personal story in one of my promotional messages to Unity of Chicago Church members. This story illustrates the effectiveness of noticing your current tension related to the challenge at hand and transforming the situation by shifting your shallow breathing patterns to deeper breathing. This story also discusses the importance of empowering self-talk and short-term goal setting.

Going from Stuck to Unstuck
Being More Resourceful in the Moment of Need

When I was six years old, I knew that I wanted to play music in whatever ways were possible. So I begged my parents for piano lessons, which they willingly gave me. Years later I played viola in the high school orchestra and went on to study at one of the best music schools in the country. Yet I never felt that I was quite in synch with the other musicians. Even though music was a core love and expression of my soul, I experienced far too many times a feeling of being lost and out of synch with my fellow musicians while performing the music.

When this happened, my shoulders would hunch up to my ears, my breath would become shallow, my cheeks would redden with embarrassment, and my internal dialogue would focus on making myself as invisible as possible.

In the interim years, I managed to attend summer music festivals, take some voice lessons, and even graduate from the Manus School of Music in New York. After that, I got married, moved from the east to Chicago, and refocused my life. Yet my love of music still lingered in my soul.

So, many years later, I found myself pulled to sing in a gospel-funk fusion choir. Within two rehearsals, our choir was engaged to sing at the opening of the Greenhouse Mall in Barrington, Illinois. The talented and ambitious choir director required us to memorize the music and follow all of his instructions to the letter. When it came time to sing the Battle Hymn of the Republic, he wanted us to clap along to the music and march in place while we sang this song as dynamically as possible. Even though I was new to the choir, I was placed in the middle of the front row. So as much as I wanted to just blend into the background, I had no other option than to do my best to get in synch with the choir – or quickly run off the stage.

But for the first few measures of the song, that old familiar sense of feeling overwhelmed, anxious, fearful, and embarrassed took over my entire being. Even though it was five decades later, I still was struggling with clapping my hands in time to the music while singing and marching.

However, I was no longer a struggling teenager/young adult and I had learned several important things along the way which helped me turn this initially trying situation into a happy, successful experience.

Here are some of the important things that helped me to turn the situation around and to go from **"I Can't"** to **"I Can"**. First and most importantly, I had to shift my awareness and change my breathing pattern from the panic-driven shallow breathing pattern to deeper hara (belly) breathing.

Once I did this, I was able to notice what possible elements could support me in going from being out of synch and feeling I was helpless and frustrated to feeling centered and resourceful. In the moment I changed my breathing, the old negative internal dialogue was also put on pause.

Instead of being at the mercy of my limiting inner script of "You just can't do this, you never could, and you never will. It's hopeless to think it will be any different now." I took charge of my thoughts and initiated positive self-talk with new messages such as "Just relax, enjoy this experience, and notice the resources available to you in this moment that help you stay in synch with the choir."

Suddenly, I was able to notice that there was a very good drummer beating out the rhythm behind us. All I really had to do was to let my hands dance in the form of clapping to his rhythm.

Next, I updated my internal script to, "It's easier than you think. All you need to do is relax in the moment. Enjoy yourself and let your senses respond to the supporting stimuli."

This helped me to set a short-term goal of just being in the moment and enjoying performing the rest of the song.

All of these decisions and actions helped me to get out of the knee-jerk survival reactions of fight, flight, and/or freeze. These actions calmed my deep limbic system by sending a clear signal to the frontal cortex of my brain. These new signals helped me maintain a proactive strategy of maintaining awareness of my breathing patterns. By changing my shallow breathing to deeper breathing, I was able to then transform my negative internal script into a positive internal script In effect; I created new meanings for this particular moment of trauma. Instead of maintaining the meaning that this is just another example of not being competent, I made it signify that I had a new opportunity to be proactive and resourceful.

How to Transform Your Breathing Patterns:

Here are the easy steps to accomplish this process:

1. Notice when you are experiencing a heightened state of tension and anxiety.

2. Consciously take a deep breath. If your hand is resting on your belly, which is also known as your hara (*www.answers.com/topic/hara-*3), you will feel your belly expanding as you take these deep breaths.

3. Once you change your shallow breathing pattern to deeper breathing, you will also be able to pause the negative thoughts that have been playing through your mind as accompaniment for your current challenging situation.

Taking audible sighs is also effective. As Jamie Smart states, in his Better Coaching Skills workshop, "Just go, 'Ah' ...Because your auditory cortex is wrapped around the other cortexes in your brain. So when you hear nice sounds, it feels good. It feels good in your body. So this is a way you can relax yourself in any situation."

According to the Guru Sri Siva, creator of Mind Science, "Ah" is the sound of creation and manifestation. (Sri Siva, *One Minute Guide* p. 45.)

3. Enhance Your Listening Skills

In this section, we explore four ways to enhance your listening skills. The four ways are:

1. Placing the "Tip of Your Tongue on the Roof of Your Mouth"
2. Accepting the Mind and Body as One Unit
3. Breathing Deeply
4. Keeping Your Focus Outward.

Place the Tip of Your Tongue on the Roof of Your Mouth, (just behind your two front teeth)

Now, why would you do that? We think 300 to 1,000 words per minute, according to some neuroscientists (*The Brain*. Dir. Richard Vaag. Darlow Smithson Productions, www.History.com). And when we are thinking these words in our head, the micro-muscles in our tongues are also moving in synch to these thoughts.

When you take your tongue and put it on the roof of your mouth, which is a little more practical than holding your tongue, you will lessen the speed of the internal monologue that is playing through your mind. If this technique doesn't totally stop your internal monologue process, it will at least slow it down.

If you are wondering exactly how to do this technique, just imagine that you are holding a drop of oil against the roof of your mouth with the tip of your tongue. This will help you to implement the technique and lessen the internal dialogue in your head. When I conduct my workshops, I like to add the following instruction to the group: "I would encourage all of you tonight, when you are beginning to share (experiences), to put your tongue on the roof of your mouth and breathe deeply."

By stilling your thoughts, you will be able to listen more intently to other people. As you do this you will be able to learn and hear more than you would have been able to do otherwise.

I asked my course participants about their experiences with the technique of placing their tongues on the roofs of their mouths while they interacted with other people. Janice shared the following story with us about her toddler-aged grandson: "It worked well, especially with my grandson, because once he starts talking he keeps going, going, going . . . Before, I would lose my patience with him. But, this time, I put my tongue on the roof of my mouth and really tried to listen more slowly than he spoke to catch some of what it was he was expressing and what it was he was doing . . . and so I was able not to get anxious about it. I felt calmer and then I was able to stop him and ask him what he had just said instead of not hearing what he was saying. And so that was new to both of us."

Breathe deeply while you are practicing your listening skills with other people.

Why? Because by shifting your breathing from shallow breaths to deeper breaths, you will be able to relax and feel more centered and present. This deeper breathing practice will also help you stop the being "stuck in your head" feeling and help you feel more connected to your body.

Other Practices that Employ Instructions for Placing of the Tip of Your Tongue on the Roof of Your Mouth Include "The Microcosmic Orbit"

There is a Taoist meditation practice that starts with opening the Microcosmic Orbit. In this procedure, one focuses on circulating one's life force through two of the most important energy channels in the body. These two channels, the Functional (Ren Mai) and the Governor (Du Mai), connect in a flowing circle going up the spine, over the head, and down the front center of the body. The front and back channel are joined to form a circuit of continuous energy flow. This circuit is called the "Microcosmic Orbit", and it is also referred to as the small heavenly cycle.

This is yin and yang in practice, connecting the masculine back channel and feminine front channel. Bringing your tongue to the roof of your mouth generates this connection. This meditation allows you to increase, recycle, and store reservoirs of chi in an energy center in your abdomen called the lower "Dan Tien." (Marie Favorito, Marie. *The Microcosmic Orbit*. The Boston Healing Tao. 2011). *(www.bostonhealingtao.com/microcosmicorbit.php).*

The tip of the tongue on the roof of the mouth is also practiced in Tai Chi, Cobra Breathing, Qi Gong, and many Yoga related practices. These various modalities help the practitioner lessen his states of stress and rejuvenate his body, mind, and spirit. So, if you have further interest in learning more about this tongue on the roof of the mouth technique, I suggest you research it further on the internet. The websites listed in the citations would be good places to start.

The Tao Bums: Tongue/Roof of Mouth

Putting the tongue to the roof of the mouth is how you connect the two main paths of the microcosmic orbit – one going up the back and around the top of the head, and the other going down the front of the chest.

Having your tongue in that position ensures that the energy can freely and safely flow through the full circuit. And as you get to higher levels and start handling more energy, having everything flow smoothly is important. *(www.thetaobums.com/index.php?/topic/13629-tongueroof-of-mouth).*

How to Do the Cobra Breathing Exercise

The Cobra Breath is a tantric breathing exercise. In essence, it is an energy-building breath. One uses breath to move kundalini energy up from the root chakra, at the base of the spine, to the crown chakra, which lies at the top of the head. The particular form of the Cobra Breath, outlined below, is used to expand consciousness, and it can lead to states of bliss and joy. Moving kundalini energy through the body is also rejuvenating for your organs and aids cellular processes.

Follow the steps below to experience the Cobra Breath:

Difficulty: Moderately Challenging

5. Sit on the edge of a chair, with the edge your buttocks resting on the seat. You may put your hands on your knees if desired. You can also sit on the floor with your back against the wall and use a pillow to support your lower back.

6. Press your tongue on the roof of your mouth. Squeeze your anal muscles or perineum (the root chakra), and hold.

7. Breathe in. As you breathe in, first feel the energy rise up from the base of your spine. It should progress to the back of your head and around the top to the

crown of your head. Keep your tongue pressed on the roof of the mouth, and make sure your anal muscles stay contracted.

8. Slowly, breathe out and make a hissing noise like a snake. As you breathe out, keep your tongue on the roof of your mouth. Your facial muscles around your jaw and lips should be contracted, almost as if you are smiling, when breathing out.

(*www.ehow.com/how_2322034_do-cobra-breathing-exercise.html#ixzz0w8xEoji7*)

The Inner Smile: A Meditation Practice

The practice of the Inner Smile is one that is found in Hindu, Buddhist, and Taoist traditions. This practice is a wonderful way to release anxiety, to balance the endocrine system, and to increase within you, feelings of loving-kindness and compassion. Here's how you do it:

4. Find a quiet place to sit, either in a straight-backed chair (sitting near the edge, with your feet parallel, and directly beneath your knees) or on the floor (in a comfortable cross-legged position, or in "hero" position, sitting back on your heels). The most important thing is for you to feel comfortable, and for your spine to be in an upright position.

5. Let your eyes gently close.

6. Take a couple of deep long breaths, and as you exhale say (either out loud or internally) "Ahhh."

7. As you exhale and say "Ahhh," feel any unnecessary tension in the face, jaw, neck, and shoulders simply melt away, like a series of thin silk scarves, flowing off of your body, down to the floor.

8. Notice a feeling of spaciousness in your mouth, as though the roof of your mouth were the dome of a temple.

9. Now let your breathing return to normal, and float the tip of your tongue upward, letting it rest gently on the roof of your mouth, right behind your upper front teeth. (You'll find a "sweet spot" that feels just perfect!).

10. Keeping your tongue lightly touching the roof of your mouth (and with your eyes still closed), allow yourself to smile . . . a very gentle, subtle smile (sort of like the Mona Lisa) . . . as though you were just smiling to yourself, for no particular reason, letting your lips fill and spread. Notice how this feels.

11. Now rest your attention (your mind's eye) at the bridge of your nose – that space on your forehead between the inner edges of your eyebrows. Notice that as you rest your attention there, energy builds.

(Whisper. *The Inner Smile: A Meditation Practice.* Yahoo! Contributor Network, P Web. 29 June 2006.) *The Inner Smile: A Meditation Practice* article link: (*www.associatedcontent.com/article/40018/ the_inner_smile_a_meditation_practice.html*)

Mind and Body are One Unit

Have you ever heard the expression, "Actions speak louder than words?" How often has a mother or girlfriend said to a young woman, "Don't just pay attention to what he says; pay attention to what he does!"

When we are willing to take in the information that is conveyed through actions and gestures, we are able to get a truer sense of who the person is, because often the gestures are related to primal limbic signals and instincts. For instance, if you are in a conversation with someone and their feet are pointing away from you, it is quite possible that this person is thinking about how they can end the conversation and make a quick exit out of the room.

Why? According to Joe Navarro, the author of *What Every Body Is Saying*, "For millions of years, the feet and legs have been the primary means of locomotion for the human species. They are the principal means by which we have maneuvered, escaped, and survived....If you want to decode the world around you and interpret behavior accurately, watch the feet and legs; they are truly remarkable and honest in the information they convey." (Navarro, *What Every Body Is Saying*, p. 54-60)

While you are listening to someone, stilling your own thoughts will make it easier to take in the total communication of the person. Often, people have been indoctrinated into not saying what is really on their minds. However, if you also watch their gestures, you will be able to understand more fully what is going on for this person.

Through my twenty some years of teaching I have observed that the mind relates to a person's conscious processing of content, while the body gestures and motions indicate the person's unconscious communications. As the developers of the Neuro-Linguistic Program have stated, our conscious minds can only take in about five to nine bits of data, while our unconscious minds are taking in everything that is happening ALL the time, even when we are sleeping and/or under anesthesia.

If you want to truly understand the people in your life, explore the following books about what our bodies are communicating simultaneously with our words during our conversations with people: *What Every Body Is Saying*, by Joe Navarro, *The Definitive Book of Body Language*, by Allyn and Barbara Pease, and *You Can Read Anyone*, by David

Lieberman. (See *Works Cited* at the end of this book for further details)

More Reasons to Breathe Deeply

Deep, rhythmic breathing expands the diaphragm muscle, the arch-shaped muscle under your lungs, increasing the lung's air pockets, invoking the relaxation response, and massaging the lymphatic system.

Breathing Exercises and the Relaxation Response

Deep breathing is the fastest way to trigger your parasympathetic nervous system, through what some practitioners call the relaxation response. Further review and analysis of research by Drs. Brown and Gerbarg resulted in the development of a new neuropsychological theory for how yogic breathing may affect the stress response system and calm the mind and body. Their recent article *Revive Yourself* in *Current Psychiatry* (Thought Rocket, May 4, 2009. www.thoughtrocket.com/2009/05/post-for-39) shows how trained deep breathing can relieve trauma symptoms.

The sympathetic nervous system, which is stimulated in times of stress and anxiety, controls your fight or flight response, including spikes in cortisol and adrenaline that can be damaging when they persist too long. Chronic stress depletes the body of nutrients and destabilizes brain and endocrine chemistry. Depression, muscle tension and pain, insulin sensitivity, gastro-intestinal (GI) issues, insomnia, and adrenal fatigue, among scores of other conditions, are all related to an overworked sympathetic nervous system. What counteracts this mechanism? The parasympathetic nervous system counteracts this mechanism.

Breath is the fastest medium by which these systems can communicate, flicking the switch from high alert to low in a matter of seconds.

Keeping Your Focus Outward

"Nature gave us one tongue and two ears so we could hear twice as much as we speak." Epictetus

When Richard Bandler, one of the developers of NLP (Neuro-Linguistic Programing), was asked how he got so good at it, he said, "I'll tell you the secret, you watch and listen."

It is human nature to go inside and find experiences that resemble the ones that you are encountering externally. NLP terms this process a *trans-derivational search*. "In NLP, a trans-derivational search (Bandler and Grinder, 1976) is essentially the process of *searching back* through one's stored memories and mental representations to find the personal reference experiences from which a current understanding or mental map has been derived." (Dilts, Robert. *Trans-derivational Morphology.* NLP University/ The Article of the Month 1999 www.nlpu.com/Articles/artic27.htm).

Yet, when you keep the tip of your tongue on the roof of your mouth, you will be able to slow down your internal thoughts and stay more focused on the person and events that are taking place in your external reality. Since trans-derivational searches are an automatic process for all human beings, make a commitment to yourself to notice when you are automatically looking for internal references to the speakers external representation, take a deep breath, maintain the position of the tip of your tongue on the roof of your mouth and gently shift your focus again to the speaker in front of you.

Eye Accessing Cues

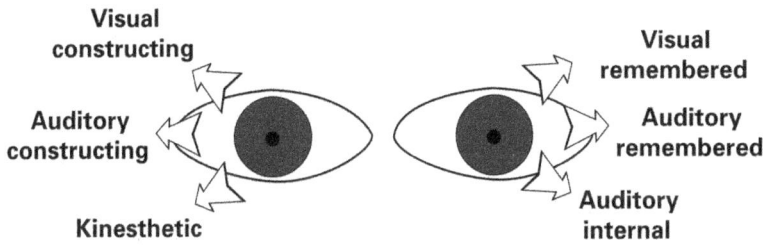

This chart demonstrates the typical "accessing eyes patterns" of the person whom you are facing. For instance, when this person's eyes shift to the upper left corner (which is your right side) this person will be accessing a visual based memory.

If the eyes of this person shift to the right, this person will be accessing constructed versus remembered data.

4. Manage Your Stress States to Become More Resourceful

The first session of the course included the following information that was presented and then discussed with, the participants:

Terry: Our beliefs create our experience of reality. We are going to watch clips of a wonderful movie about *The Brain* (A&E/History Channel, *The Brain,* DVD, 2008) because the brain is what makes the mental constructs. It's where the shadow beliefs are; it's where we have installed survival mechanisms and it's where fear has resided.

Key points from the video:

> The brain, which controls every aspect of our lives, has doubled in size as humans have evolved. It weighs about three pounds, but consumes 20% of our body's energy.
>
> The oldest part of the brain, the brain stem, governs vital functions such as heart rate, digestion, and blood pressure without conscious intervention.
>
> Evolving more recently, the limbic system and especially the amygdala, govern feelings, including fear (one of the simplest and strongest emotions). The video goes on to talk about how at the Navy Seals Special Warfare Command in San Diego recruits are put through special training to change the way their brains react to fear.

Terry: A couple of things here: I would not necessarily have chosen warriors to demonstrate this point; however, we are probably all warriors in one way or another and also we know that the government puts a lot of money into the military. Right? So, that means that they also put a lot of money into research on how to train people to be more resourceful under stress.

And when I was teaching at a local college, one of the biggest conditions that people kept telling me about was their stress and anxiety. I think that these feelings of anxiety are just part of our times. Stress levels have increased for many people. This presentation will help you gain new and effective keys to help you manage and decrease stress as well as experience a greater sense of calm, peace, relaxation, and vitality.

Points from the video:

> The Navy turned to neuroscience to answer the question of why one person is able to overcome fear while another isn't. They found that the highly interconnected amygdala responds to information from our senses and triggers fear responses such as sweating, fainting, freezing, or fleeing.

Terry: Does that make sense to people? The other thing that is important to people is that the amygdala and limbic system react like that (snap of the fingers) – at lightning speed. And then the signals that go on to the prefrontal cortex are slower. So the Navy Seal trainers do a lot of training to help the recruits be more resourceful and to reduce unnecessary reactions and to increase the speed of the communication from the limbic system to the prefrontal cortex.

Our bodies experience the world through our senses. People and things become associated with feelings and sensations. And something interesting that I learned from studying Dr. Amen's work is that the only sense that goes immediately to the limbic system is the sense of... Does anybody know what it is?

Lila: Fear?

Terry: Smell. Have you ever experienced a situation where you smell something and it immediately evoked memories of a past situation? So if you want to quickly create a greater sense of calm, bring in more good smells to your environment. I have a diffuser for this.

Myra: Smell goes into the limbic system?

Terry: Yes, the limbic system.

Points from the video:

> The prefrontal cortex is the most recently evolved part of our brain. It is where conscious, rational thought is processed. It is what makes us human.
>
> A major scientific discovery in fear research is that information from our senses reaches the amygdala twice as fast as it reaches the prefrontal cortex.

Terry: That's what I said, but it is good to see it. One of the things that I am doing tonight, as you may have noticed, is that I am presenting this work in a whole-brained way – you are getting the visuals, the music, the concepts, and the language. And the prefrontal cortex is what is involved in language. As you can see from this video, the other parts of the brain are the older parts. And that is why I am saying that it is very important to pay attention to the signals that you are getting from the older parts of your brain and body.

As we evolved, we developed speech, and started using words to give expression to problems and situations. That is why we call them mental constructs. So now that we have verbal expression, it is really important to start being aware of how we are verbalizing our problems and experiences, because that is also a way that we are setting our internal computers.

Points from the video:

> Under normal conditions, the brain communicates with the body via electrical signals (nerve impulses). But when we are under stress, the amygdala causes stress hormones like cortisol to be

released. These increase breathing, heart rate, and blood pressure, sharpen the senses, and make us less sensitive to pain, thus preparing us for action.

Terry: The military marine trainers take their trainees through a test, where they have to stay under water to the point where they feel like they have no more oxygen. And when they are at that point they have to be resourceful. The training is to help them strengthen their ability to think in high stress life-death situations and surmount all obstacles.

Points from the video:

Eric Potterat – a Command Psychologist of the Navy Seals – discussed what he calls the BIG FOUR techniques:

A. Goal setting

B. Mental Rehearsal

C. Self-Talk

D. Arousal Control.

In particular, scientists think that goal setting assists the frontal lobes in bringing order to chaos and in keeping the amygdala in check.

Terry: That's what I was talking about. That's why I also said in the beginning that we are goal setting, goal-seeking human beings. And the goal setting can also help us get through tough, stressful times. And goal setting can also help us to be more participatory and just experience more in whatever situation we are in. When we are able to set a clear goal – and have a clear idea of the outcome we want, and also have an idea of how we know we have it – then we are really able to be more vibrant, more participatory, and truly fully engaged in every experience we are in.

Points from the video:

> "The second technique, mental rehearsal or visualization, consists of running through an activity in your mind." (*The Brain.*)

Terry: We've all done that - right? We've meditated and we've visualized something unfold. So that is part of the picture. And it's definitely one of the four keys that we are talking about. And another part certainly is to realize when you are having a negative visualization and to transform it into a positive, empowering one.

Points from the video:

> The third technique, self-talk, helps focus on one's thoughts. 'One speaks to oneself an average of three hundred to one thousand words a minute.' (*The Brain.*)

Terry: Tongue on the roof of the mouth!

Points from the video:

> "If these words are positive instead of negative – "Can do" instead of "Can't" – they help override the fear signals coming from the amygdala." (*The Brain.*)

Terry: The frontal lobes are always on, so our mind has the tendency to slip back into negative self-talk, like, "I'm gonna fail," or "What am I doing here?" or "I didn't practice enough." What you want to do is to replace those disempowering thoughts with empowering thoughts.

So, one of the things I had in mind when I announced this course was the concept of going from: "I can't" to "I can!" For most people, when they are talking about "I can't", there really is an "I can". They just may not have accessed their resourcefulness yet. So, just turn to somebody and say, "You too can go from 'I can't' to 'I can'."

We are a "can-do" group.

Points from the video:

"Breathing is a great focusing strategy." *(The Brain.)*

Terry: We talked about breath in the beginning.

Points from the video:

Due to the powerfulness of signals from the amygdala, arousal control by itself doesn't work very well; however, the Big Four techniques enable one to better deal with the fear they are feeling. (This can significantly increase Navy Seal trainees' pass rate.)

Terry: What I would like to do is to just have you say something that you experienced that you had not experienced before. It could be an insight, a feeling, and a thought that you hadn't understood before or even considered. Who wants to go first?

Edna: I would say self-talk. The "I can't" to "I can".

Todd: A negative belief can have a positive intention.

Terry: Definitely. It has a positive purpose. So it may not feel positive, but it's been there to keep you alive. And yes, the positive self-talk is very important, because a lot of times when we are saying something limiting to ourselves, we are just replaying imprinted negative messages from earlier, more chaotic times in our lives. At that time, we took it into our unconscious mind without filtering it out of our systems. We might have been young. We might have been sick or tired or in a state of chaos. So this is the time right now to start clearing those "I Can'ts" away to live the best life you can live, because all of us – you, me, and everyone here is capable of far more than we thought we were capable of. We are really magnificent human beings.

Megan: I like the information that it is not all or nothing. You can really keep sending the love, but call back your energy and let that be enough.

Terry: You are calling back your energy. Often when somebody has fallen in love with a person they fall in love with the entire person. And people sometimes give away those parts that the person fell in love with.

The action of calling back those parts of yourself that you may have given away to a loved one, will not diminish your loved one, but it will help you restore your own energy levels. Whatever may have been depleted on the very basic level of energy can be fully recovered by utilizing the process of recapitulation.

Greg: We have the power to change our thoughts and ourselves.

Terry: Yes we do. Thank you.

Joy: I just got – from watching that clip – some ideas about that instinctive part that goes into fear. Let's say that we'll assume a goal and then that fear comes up. If we can breathe through that fear and let the cortex take over and get a little more rational as soon as possible, we can do better. I also just watched myself go through a whole cycle of being willing to do something and then...

Gloria: I have to say that the tongue on the roof of the mouth is powerful. You had shown me a brief version of (see *Chapter Six*) before. But there are so many times when people are talking, especially if I am going to be expected to say something in a few minutes. And I am sitting there and I nod, and at the same time I just say whatever is in my mind in the moment, but during this talk I was keeping my tongue on the roof of my mouth and it really did make a difference in terms of focusing on and hearing what other people were saying, instead of hearing this loop of self-talk.

Terry: Wonderful. Thank you.

Cassy: Self-talk. I find that I have a lot of that in the morning because I am busiest in the morning so my thoughts are going fifty thousand words a minute. If I just keep dwelling on my negative thoughts, it's harder for me to get through everything I have to do, but I find, the more I move, the less prevalent they are. Those thoughts go away as I am moving.

Terry: Remember, the mind and body are one unit and that is a way for them to work together...Anybody else?

Tom: I like your emphasis on breath because breath is a connection to people.

Terry: Yes, it is... Now we are coming to the completion of this session. Some homework if you should decide to accept this mission!

Practice deep breathing, because this is for you to feel resourceful, calm and energized, knowing that we can take in the energy kind of like a plant that takes in sunlight. We can also take in chi and oxygen. We can help ourselves replenish.

Keep a journal.

Talk to somebody this week and let this person know what is still occurring for you. If you remember I said in the beginning, that these processes would keep going during the week. Your mind got you here, but it was also your unconscious that said, "Hmm I might not be sure about being here, but here I am." So there were many factors operating in bringing you here (to this course and this book).

And I just want to thank you for your participation and knowing that you are magnificent people and there are going to be some wonderful things that happen to you this week as a result of being open and willing.

Now that we have gone over some of the transcript of the first session of the B.E.S.T. course, here are some further thoughts and processes related to the BIG FOUR techniques for dealing with response to stress [*The Brain*]:

Goal setting

1. Mental Rehearsal
2. Self-Talk

3. Arousal Control

4. Goal setting.

In the video, *The Brain*, short-term goal setting was discussed as something to help us get through tough, stressful times. Goal setting should also be done on a daily, weekly, monthly, yearly, and longer-term basis. Studies have shown that people who set personal and professional goals are more likely to be happier and more successful. Many people have written about the power of goal setting, including NLP practitioners, coaches, teachers, and leaders in many walks of life.

So let's take a step-by-step approach to creating a successful goal structure and plan:

- Get clear on something you want to experience. Make the goal a tangible event. Some of my personal and professional goals have included: teaching a series of classes, writing a book, gaining a graduate degree, losing weight, gaining coaching and bodywork certification, etc.

- Create a step-by-step plan to achieve this goal. Don't worry if you don't put down all the steps at this point because the steps will become clearer along the way.

- Set a life-line/time-line completion/realization date to your goal. Set dates for completion of each step. Even if you have to shift your dates to earlier or later dates, it is still helpful to have a target date to accomplish your goal.

- Write out descriptions of how you will recognize that you have accomplished your goal. Include signposts for each step along the way.

- Set up a support team that will also hold the vision of you successfully completing this goal. This group may include friends, mastermind groups, prayer groups, and professional association groups. Another effective way of setting up a support system is to find an "accountability buddy" where you check in with each other on a daily or weekly basis. During this check-in time, you go over what you have accomplished, what you still need to do, and ways to move through any and all blocks that may be in the way of achieving your current goals.

- **Present View (PV) to Best View (BV) of Your Situation:** Take a piece of paper and draw a line vertically through the middle of it. On the left side draw out in simplistic stick figure forms your present view of your situation relating to your goal. On the right side of the paper draw out the best view of your completed goal. It should be about ten times better than your present view, so that your conscious mind accepts this goal as doable.

- Take a few minutes and meditate on the completion of this goal. Look for and understand what the bridge may be between these two views. For me, sometimes this bridge looks like hands clasped together in prayer to symbolize the divine assistance of God's loving presence in my life and my life's goal.

2. Mental Rehearsal/Visualization

Post your PV to BV picture in a place where you will see it every day. This place could be on the frame of your computer, or your bathroom mirror or refrigerator door. By placing this image in a location where you unconsciously see it every day, you will be sending subliminal messages to your mind.

Mental rehearsal can also involve playing positive internal scripts and movies inside your head. So many times people replay disaster stories rather than empowering stories because of their childhood conditioning. However now that you are an adult, you can take control of these stories. By replaying positive stories, you will redirect your mind to look for positive results in your life.

3. Self-Talk

Most of us have been given negative scripts during our childhood years. Yet as adults we have a chance to transform these scripts into more empowering self-talk. We will discuss this in greater detail in the following chapters, especially when we explore the scripts that are played out in the Drama Triangle (see *Chapter Five*).

4. Arousal Control

This is the term, utilized by the Navy Seals to help them handle their stress responses. The biggest aspect of arousal control is how you can use breath management to shift from shallow breathing to deep breathing to calm the limbic system.

Summary

This chapter is devoted to the Four Keys of Stress Management – because once you begin to manage your stress responses, you will be able to tap into your deeper resources for self-improvement.

5. Homework Exercises

The most important practices to master this week are:

1. Breath Management.

2. Creation of a "before and after" picture and posting it in a familiar place.

3. Write out two well-formed goals/outcomes:

    - A short-term goal for the week.

    - A long-term goal to be accomplished within six to ten weeks.

Chapter Two: Empower Your Beliefs

1. Introduction

It is my experience that beliefs are verbalizations/mental concepts that represent the following:

- Meanings I have assigned to specific events in my life.

- Values I have inherited, as well as formulated on my own about various aspects of life.

- Identities that I have taken on in this lifetime.

What precede the formulation of beliefs are feelings, interactions, and experiences. Until I actually formulate words for these feelings about, perceptions of, actions regarding, and responses to various life experiences, I am not actually dealing in the realm of experience. So to take this thought to the next level of exploration, I would also say that words are symbols representing specific perceptions and attitudes about my life experiences and other people's life experiences.

The following personal story represents these ideas about beliefs:

About two decades ago, I was struggling with the painful ending of my ten-year marriage and the challenging task of completing my divorce from my first husband. Although there was already a new man in my life, I was still having a tough time completing my divorce. By the time I participated in a Quantum Consciousness Psychology weekend course offered by the brilliant author and teacher, Stephan Wolinsky, I was in my third year of the expensive and trying separation and divorce process.

After the completion of Stephan's course, I agreed to participate in a weekly support group that worked with twenty-two identity questions introduced in the course. By the third practice session I decided to explore my identity related to being indecisive in finalizing my divorce.

These identity questions explore the role models in our lives. It didn't seem that my mother or father modeled indecisiveness, so I looked to the generation before them and realized that this identity was related to my grandmothers. When my respective grandfathers passed away, both of my grandmothers remained single and never looked at or dated another man. That part of their lives was over.

Somehow, I had taken on the idea that divorce meant that I would never date or marry another man, even though I was much younger than my grandmothers were when their marriages ended. Somehow, their choices had elicited an unconscious and irrational fear response in me.

Going through the identity process instantly dissolved the fear and belief that ending my marriage meant that a certain part of my life was permanently over.

This realization dissolved the fear that had been stopping me from completing my divorce for three years. Now I was able to see the absurdity of this fear and I completed the divorce and signed the papers within ten days of making that discovery about the hidden beliefs and fears related to those unconscious fears.

Stuart Wilde, who led a preparation session for his fire-walking event that was included in his Warrior Weekend training course, stated that the word FEAR was an acronym for:

False

Evidence

Appearing

Real.

If we are not sure that we have fears that are holding us back, it is important to learn how to find the hidden fears that are limiting our choices. Then we must access the beliefs that are associated with these underlying feelings of fear, anxiety, unresolved grief, helplessness and worthlessness. Once we name the beliefs, we can deconstruct them and take the energy that was dedicated to holding them in place and apply it toward constructing empowering beliefs that propel our lives forward so we may live the most magnificent life possible.

2. Definitions of Beliefs

Here are some standard definitions for the word "belief" or "believe":

> The Greek word for believe is pisteuo (pist-yoo'o) and means to have faith, to trust in. To believe, as in faith, is far different than simply to believe something. For instance, the devils believe God exists, and fear him, but it does not save them. The scriptures use the terms to "believe in" and "to believe on". To believe on connotes trust. To believe in simply agrees that something is.

("Believe" Answers.com *wiki.answers.com/Q/ What_is_greek_meaning_of_the_word_believe*)

Belief is the psychological state in which an individual holds a proposition or premise to be true. (*en.wikipedia.org/wiki/Belief*)

A state or habit of mind in which trust of confidence is placed in some person or thing.

A thing believed; especially: a tenet or body of tenets held by a group.

A conviction of the truth of some statement or the reality of some being or phenomenon especially when based on examination of evidence.

(*www.merriam-webster.com*).

Look at the words that are common to these definitions, such as: conviction of truth, state, and/or habit of mind.

Here are some of the definitions and perceptions of my students regarding the topic of beliefs from my transcript of my six-week Spring Course in 2010.

Terry: What are your ideas about beliefs?

Todd: Can I say something?

Terry: Yes.

Todd: A belief is only a thought you keep thinking.

Edna: A program.

Todd: An experience we keep experiencing.

Greg: A conditioned habit.

Janice: An entity.

Lila: A belief can be a cage.

Joy: A belief can be liberation.

Todd: A belief brings emotions with it.

3. Key Components of Beliefs

I presented the following two key components of beliefs in this class, and called for comments from the students:

Terry: It is really important to understand in belief work that there are two aspects to all beliefs:

    1. **The Content** – which is represented in the conscious mind in the form of story & linguistic constructs.

    2. **The Structure** – which is represented in the unconscious mind in the form of sensory perceptions & associations.

Have you ever had the experience of somebody telling you the same story over and over again? Have the faces, names and places changed, but has the story remained the same?

Lila: In the movies.

Terry: Yes, in the movies. Has anybody had this experience in real life?

Joy: Well, I have a friend who – even though different people are involved – the overall story that always flows through is, "I'm so stressed out. I can't handle life." It's always different faces, different people, and different situations, but it's always the same belief that underlies it.

Terry: And it is probably hard to keep hearing it over and over again, isn't it?

Joy: Well, it's painful to experience. Through apathy, it's hard to hear it. And my lack of patience plays into it.

Terry: This is very much human nature.

Todd: "I don't have a college education; therefore, I'm limited." And that's a belief that I have thought and I keep thinking. And that's a belief that is reinforced all around me. If you don't go to school, you don't make a decent wage. If you don't have an education, you're not going anywhere. They have comparisons and charts that keep validating that.

Terry: Well, that's a great example of something – and that's a concept of:

"What the Thinker thinks, the Prover proves." If that's the belief that has been imprinted in your psyche, then you are going around saying, "I don't have a college degree, and so I can only do this." You are carrying this belief into all sorts of situations. And you are experiencing the same thing over and over. Does that make sense? So that's what we are here to do.

Todd: Attracting the same situations.

Myra: You attract what you believe.

Terry: And that is something that all human beings do, because it has helped us survive up until this point.

Greg: I was talking to my partner Carla here, and one of the things that came up was acceptance. And it reminds me that whenever I have a thought that may not always be productive, at least in my mind and in my thinking, what makes it worse, is judging it. So instead of judging it and making it wrong, it's better to go, "OK, I had that thought, observe it, accept it, love it, however you want to do that, and get it to transform, rather than making it wrong.

Terry: And even thank the judgment, because somebody taught you to judge. Most of these skills we have learned, whether they are skills that make us happy or skills that keep us unhappy –somehow we learned them because when we were babies and first came into this earth plane, we first started modeling crawling, etc. Do you remember those times? Touch your chin. Just this simple act of touching your chin and learning that "Touch your chin," means this gesture was something you had to learn in steps. You had to learn the words; then you had to learn to model the gesture. So you are putting that together. We have done that for many things that evoke good feelings and uncomfortable feelings, all sorts of feelings.

Now the psyche loves stories. So we tell stories because it keeps us entertained. It entertains other people. It also shows us how to evolve. It shows us that we can get through challenging times. And it's a way of communicating.

The structure of the unconscious is something that has been operating at a core level. And that is really where my questions and study have been directed. How do we get to those core structures? And how do we thank them? How do we deconstruct them and harness the energy to apply it to empowering thoughts and activities, so that maybe a person would say, "I don't have a college degree, but I have gumption. I've got intelligence. I've got originality. I know that with all these qualities, I can do something that is going to help people and be profitable and exciting." There are ways to turn things around, to expand our perceptions and experiences with them. That's what we are here to do.

Your unconscious mind takes things literally and listens to everything you say. For instance, when you say, "I just can't shake this feeling," your unconscious mind takes this message literally and continues to hold onto the 'unshakable' feeling.

Therefore, it is more effective to direct your unconscious mind to shake off the feeling by saying, "OK, I'm willing to shake off this feeling." You might even want to physically shake the feelings out of your body. [That's what we did in this class - we got up and shook the feelings out of our bodies.]

And it's very important to remember that the mind and body operate as one system! I also want to say that our bodies, our unconscious, have been operating for a longer time in evolution than our minds, our mental constructs. And problems are basically mental constructs. And it has to do with what we are representing with the externals in our internal maps. So that is what we are going to work on.

Todd: It seems as though our unconscious mind is like the disk in the computer, storing our experiences.

Terry: The hard drive. Sure.

Todd: The hard drive, storing lifetime after lifetime. But it's not our higher self.

Terry: That is something that we will look at more at another time. What is important to know in this moment is that the past, the present, the future are happening all at this point because we are talking about the past from right here. And we are talking about the future from right here.

There is a way to look at a timeline and be able to work through whatever we feel that has been creating blocks for us. Does that make sense?

Todd: Yes.

4. Key Points About Beliefs

Beliefs are mechanisms that sort and filter data. They are decisions that we have made about experiences and things based on external events and internal feelings and representations.

Beliefs are generalizations. In some situations we want to keep those generalizations. For instance if we are driving on a road and we see a red light hanging from a pole, we want to say, "Yeah, that's means stop before the white lines and the cross walk. The generalizations have a quality and innate intention of helping us. We have chosen them to help us survive. There are situations where the generalizations are limiting our experiences of feeling more energy, more vitality, more creativity, more optimism, more purposefulness, more love whatever it is for you.

Beliefs are meant to give us a sense of certainty in an uncertain world. It is one of the reasons we construct and tell stories to each other as well as to ourselves. We want to make sense out of the chaos. And as human beings we like certainty. We don't like to have our thought systems rattled too much unless we are in some place where we are really motivated in the moment. We also create beliefs to help us make decisions: "Oh, a red light. I think I will stop. I see a camera at the top of that red light. I choose to stop before the white lines in order to not experience adverse consequences."

Beliefs have sensory and linguistic representations. Again, we are talking about the sensory as the unconscious, which is related to our body and is always awake. Right now you are taking in certain concepts mentally; however, your unconscious and your body are taking in the sensations, the feelings, and the experiences on a deeper level so that when you leave here and go home over the days, nights, and weeks, you will integrate a lot of these ideas and processes and have these ideas and processes help you move into the place you want to be in your life.

When one sensory representation changes, the other sensory representations will also change. When we alter and change visual, kinesthetic, or auditory elements of the internal maps, everything is altered.

The Linguistic Structure of a belief can be described as either:

- A *causes* B.
- A *means* B.

"Whenever I come home, he is always . . . . ." (Fill in the blank.) Making the event of coming home and seeing the person in a certain way means . . . . (They are acting in a loving or unloving way). Notice the meanings that you assign to specific events, objects, relationships, and people.

"His criticism causes me to be angry." There may have been a time when giving that situation that meaning helped you survive, stay out of the fray, out of anger or danger, whatever it is. Yet, that meaning has become a generalization and limiting belief that has been carried into other situations and may be limiting your current life and circumstances.

We are going to work on finding those generalizations and take them apart to see if they should really apply to our lives – and when they are no longer applicable to our lives and serving us in positive ways.

Lila: Do you think people fear giving up that internal dialogue because if they have no internal dialogue, then what do they have?

Terry: Exactly. They have grown accustomed to it. That is the sense of the familiar.

Lila: There is a comfort, even if it is a negative.

Terry: Right. So we are going to find out about that internal dialogue and beliefs. We are going to do it through exploring stories, family themes, cultural and community themes. We are also going to increase our awareness of language patterns. We are going to spend more time looking at behavioral patterns. And we are going to notice the meanings we have assigned to things.

We are also going to be aware of gestures, because gestures have a whole language of their own. Has anybody noticed that? Yeah. So we have been conditioned to disregard them. Then we go, "Why did that person do that?" Even if we had a gut feeling about it, we have been conditioned to negate that feeling. However, I am here to say that it is time to acknowledge your gut feelings and all of your feelings and intuitions.

Just to talk about how we take in data and information – there are hundreds and millions of bits of information coming at us all the time. I really recommend strengthening your central nervous system to be able to handle more of it and handle it better.

Because our conscious minds can only handle about four to nine bits of data at time, we have come up with a system to discern which data to bring into our conscious mind in the moment.

Filters

This system involves filters of:

1   Deletion

2   Distortion

3   Generalization.

Has anybody ever had an experience of not being able to find his or her keys?

Group: Yeah.

Terry: That is a conscious deletion. Then what do you say when you can't find your keys and you are looking for them?

Myra: Alzheimer's.

Terry: Do you continue to say, "I can't find them. I can't find them"? Well if you continue chanting that message, your brain will think that and your "prover" will prove that you can't find them. So I recommend you start saying, "I can find them. I can find them. I can win. I can win. This will open up more constructive and positive possibilities for you.

Distortion is similar. We focus on one aspect and delete the rest. If we are having a conversation with a friend in a restaurant, we let all the other information and people fall away and fade into the background, when we are zeroed in. And that is a type of distortion.

Generalization words also create a limited perspective of a situation or relationship. Some generalization word examples are the words: "always" and "never". For instance, when you say something to the effect of, "Sam is always late for," you have projected a filter on Sam that confines your view of him as always being late. Thus, it makes it more difficult for you to bring out in Sam his ability to be early or on time; instead it is quite possible that he will continue to live into your example of him being "always late".

Have you ever noticed that when you get together with family members many of these filters keep being reactivated by your loved ones. For example, even if you have changed your behavior patterns of being late to business appointments, you still might experience being habitually late for family functions because your earlier childhood lateness filters are still present in your subconscious mind. Another example is the way adults will be treated by and act toward their parents (i.e., like children).

It is possible that all of these behaviors can serve us well – even the behaviors of being late – for instance, if it helps you avoid an accident on the expressway. However, there are times when it is good to look at these filters and related behavior patterns and decide if we want to keep them or let them go.

We take in information through the filtering system and we give it a map, just like there are maps of

	Chicago. Have any of you seen the maps of Chicago? It's a grid right?
Group:	Yeah.
Terry:	This map is not the actual streets. But it's going to help you make your way around the city of Chicago.

So the maps are important and when we begin to change the maps, we may need an update to know if there has been construction or a change in the lanes and traffic patterns, so that we are able to be adaptable to the current situation. And the same thing is true of the internal representations we utilize in our lives.

Now when we make these internal maps, they elicit an emotional response, indicating whether the situation is safe or unsafe. This affects our physiology, and based on that we make decisions and choose behaviors. This happens very quickly, but it is good to just break it down.

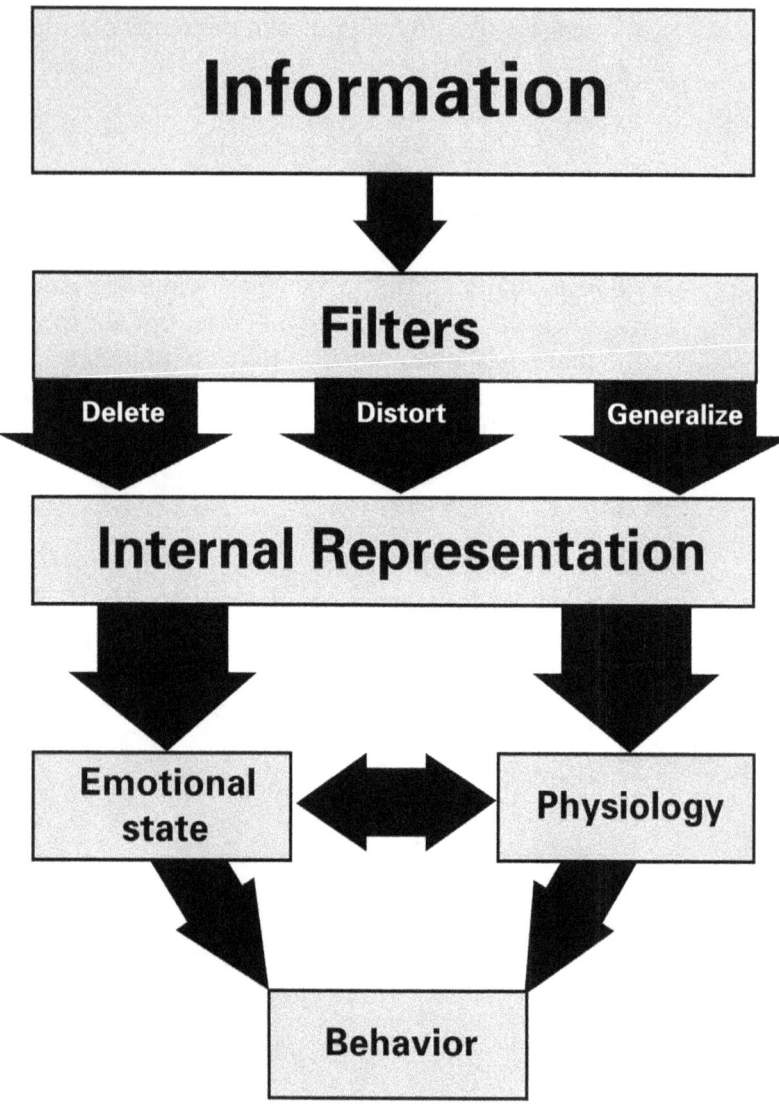

5. Factors Affecting The Formation Of Beliefs

Factors that influence the formation of our beliefs:

12. Bio-Survival Mechanisms, Physiological States, and Neurotransmitters

13. Identity Beliefs (see the section on this later in this chapter)

14. Experiential Evidence

15. Conversational Hypnosis

16. Beliefs Conveyed Through Our Speech Patterns.

In this section, we will focus on the first of these factors.

From the moment we are born, our bodies have specific biological needs that must be met to ensure our survival. As babies, we do not have words to speak our needs. Instead of speaking our needs we express our needs through smiles, gurgles, cries, yawns, and other physical gestures. Once we learn to speak we have better ways to express our needs, but we still have biological needs that must be met for our survival. We need water, food, shelter, and comfort.

Our well-being is dependent upon these needs being met. Our caregivers are doing their best to meet their own survival needs as well as to find a way to meet the needs of those who are dependent on their care. During our formative childhood years, we have varying experiences related to getting our needs met. Depending on our environment, we experience a sense of ease and safety in expressing and fulfilling these biological survival-oriented needs. Or we experience an environment of uncertainty where our needs might be mocked, ignored, criticized, and in general invalidated. And if we experience dis-ease in communicating our needs, we develop fewer direct ways to get these needs met.

Our brains are complex and remarkable organs that take on the task of recording every detail of our lives. Our brains keep our bodies functioning well. When we feel depleted in our body, our brain also reflects depletion in its functioning systems. Our thoughts, beliefs, and feelings are directly affected by states of physical and mental depletion. Negative thoughts of hopelessness, helplessness, and/or worthlessness are more likely to surface in our thinking processes when we are physically and mentally depleted.

So the first thing to do is to notice your energy levels and thoughts. Then it is important to take effective action to replenish your energy and sense of well-being.

According to Dr. Daniel Amen, MD., and Dr. David E. Smith, MD., there are four neurotransmitters that help transmit messages of well-being to the brain and are essential parts of the brain/body reward system. These four neuro-transmitters are:

- Dopamine
- Serotonin
- GABA
- Endorphins.

Scientists have discovered that dopamine, serotonin and adrenalin levels are elevated during the initial phase of falling in love.

("Your Amazing Brain." The Welcome Trust. *www.youramazingbrain.org/lovesex/sciencelove.htm*).

Dopamine

Raised dopamine levels also elevate the sense of pleasure in a person's mind and body. Dopamine levels can be naturally activated through the activities of drinking green tea and participating in aerobic exercise.

Although I am not much of a green tea drinker, I have found that when I mix green tea with either juice or coffee, I still experience the beneficial effects of green tea.

Serotonin

Serotonin helps people feel less anxious, less worried, less depressed, less combative, and more flexible in their thinking processes. The amino acid: l-tryptophan helps raise the level of serotonin in the brain, as does aerobic exercise.

Many people associate l-tryptophan with feeling tired after indulging in a sumptuous Thanksgiving meal, because turkey contains a large amount of l-tryptophan. However most people who complain of feeling tired because of the l-tryptophan in the turkey are not taking into account all of the sugar and related carbohydrates that they just consumed by eating the breads, the turkey stuffing and the sugary pumpkin and pecan pies with ice cream. I personally have found that when I just eat turkey without all of the fattening trimmings, I feel energized and experience a greater sense of well-being related to the increased levels of serotonin in my brain.

GABA

GABA (aka Gamma-aminobutyric acid) is known to help calm and relax the brain and body. If a person has experienced a recent traumatic situation, it is likely that their GABA levels have been depleted. The effect of this depletion will be evident in the increased activity in the limbic system, which is likely to create an increased sense of sadness and anxiety in the person.

It is possible to ingest a GABA supplement to increase the level of GABA in the brain. Other supplements that also increase GABA in the brain are lemon balm, kava-kava, valerian and magnesium. I have also found that taking a good calcium supplement that contains magnesium can also be a helpful way to insure a greater night's relaxation and sleep. The magnesium helps the body absorb the calcium.

Endorphins

The fourth type of neurotransmitter, endorphins, is also related to a feeling of increased pleasure in the brain/body's reward system cycles. It also lessens the feeling of pain. Imbibing cocoa (without the excess sugar additives) or dl-phenylalanine, along with exercising aerobically, will increase the levels of endorphins in the body.

As you can see from this section about how to maintain and increase the level of these important feel-good neurotransmitters, aerobic exercise is an important way of creating a greater sense of well-being.

Some students have objected to this advice based their concerns about their physical challenges such as weakened knees and joints. Yet, for those people who are not physically able to experience increased physical exercise, it is possible to learn effective breathing techniques that also naturally increase the oxygen levels in the body, thereby increasing the circulation in the brain and giving the body and brain the same results as a good aerobic exercise would have supplied to the person. One of my favorite DVDs for this sort of stationary workout routine is titled: *Fat Free Yoga - Lose Weight & Feel Great For Beginners & Beyond w/ Ana Brett & Ravi Singh*. (*www.raviana.com*).

Anna Bret and Ravi Singh are highly respected kundalini practitioners and teachers. I have been utilizing their kundalini programs since 1983. If I am experiencing any sort of misalignment in my spine, I find that their kundalini yoga DVDs will help me correct and heal the misalignments. I would also like to add that if I were experiencing any sort of misalignment in my body, I would also look to see if there are any sort of distortion and misaligned beliefs in my relationships and thinking processes. Also, refer to "Sit and Be Fit" on PBS and DVDs.

6. *Identity Beliefs*

Our identify beliefs can be formed because of the influence of family values, community values, peer pressure, authority figures and media messages.

As I mentioned in the story about finding a successful resolution to my first marriage's drawn-out separation and divorce process, finding the hidden identities was important. With the permission of Steven Wolinsky, here are the identity questions that helped me find the hidden limiting beliefs:

Identity Questions by Stephen Wolinsky:

17. Which identity came first?

18. Who modeled that identity for you?

19. Have you ever used "XXX" identity to manage something?

20. What idea could an "XXX" identity use to make himself feel right and another feel wrong?

21. By an "XXX" identity having that idea, what does it get him into and out of?

22. By an "XXX" identity having that idea, what problem or confusion does it help him solve?

23. Where in your body do you experience "XXX" identity?

24. Can you adopt that stance?

25. By an "XXX" identity having that idea, how does it help him avoid domination or dominate others?

26. What idea could this "XXX" identity use to make himself feel right and make a "YYY" feel wrong?

27. What idea could this "XXX" use to make himself feel wrong?

28. What lie could the "XXX" identity tell the "YYY" identity?

29. What lie could the "XXX" tell himself?

30. What philosophy could an "XXX" identity come up with?

31. Why would anyone want to take on an "XXX" identity?

32. What could a "XXX" identity do to a "YYY" identity?

33. What could an "XXX" identity withhold from a "YYY" identity?

34. What could an "XXX" identity from himself?

35. In order to give up this "XXX" identity, what would have to happen?

36. In order to give up this "XXX" identity, what would have to stop happening?

37. If you wanted this "XXX" identity, could you have it?

38. If you wanted this "YYY" identity, could you have it?

It is my experience that the first four of the foregoing questions help you to establish the most important identity to work on in the session, while the remaining questions are recurrent questions of the form: Why would a "XXX" identity come up with that idea (that lie, that philosophy)? These questions are ones that you may want to keep asking yourself more than once and continue asking even after you have established the answers to the first four questions.

Observer, Consciousness, Emptiness

A helpful explanation of this process of exploring identities can be found in Wolinsky's book: *The Way of the Human: The Quantum Psychology Notebooks, Volume II. The False Core and the False Self.*

Often we unconsciously take on beliefs that are spoken or displayed through specific actions and lifestyle choices of the people we value. These beliefs can be imparted to us through family members, teachers, authority figures, community members, friends, and partners. We also pick up beliefs through the ever-present media formats in our lives: TV, radio, movies, magazines, billboards, and Internet-based messages (in the various websites and webcasts).

It is also possible that physical, mental, emotional, and/or spiritual challenges lead people to create specific ideas, rules and beliefs to avoid such challenges in their present and future lives. For instance, if a person had a difficult, unsettling experience while walking in a snowstorm, they might decide to minimize the number of times they would have to go out into a snowstorm. Or they may come up with rules for walking in snowstorms such as dressing in warmer clothing, taking cell phones with them, or limiting the amount of time that they spend outside during inclement weather. Although this example might not apply to everyone, just take a look at your own life and notice what sort of decisions you have made and beliefs you have created that are related to stressful and challenging times in your life.

A clue to identifying these beliefs might be found by noticing the filter words you have included in your decisions. For example, I was reluctant to put a seventeen and a half year old pet to sleep, despite the advice of well meaning vets and friends. Yet, when I really took into account the amount of suffering this little animal endured only to extend his life a few more months, I decided that I would *never* put another animal through such an ordeal and compromised standard of living.

My father had a belief that his life was only worth living if he could maintain a good quality of life. The last three years of his life were focused on a struggle with colon cancer. When he finally sold his boat, I knew that he had decided that the end of his life was near because for him quality of life included being able to motorboat and fish in Florida.

It seems that people pick up beliefs about health and aging by consciously and unconsciously observing their family members, loved ones, and environmental messages. The media messages contribute to the changing of beliefs by conveying messages such as "Fifty is the New Forty" (e.g., see: *www.fiftyisthenewforty.net*).

7. Hidden Beliefs

If you are experiencing stress over certain aspects of your life, start noticing what you are telling yourself about this particular condition, problem, and/or situation. This will help you find the limiting beliefs that have been operating in your psyche to keep this condition, problem and/or situation in place.

For instance, you might automatically replay a negative message such as, "You always screw up buddy," when you get into a jam. Notice this message, have compassion for yourself; thank it; call back the energy that you were utilizing to hold it in place; release the thought; and then make a new choice to say something to yourself; such as, "You have the ability to find your way out of whatever jam you experience." Whatever you are saying to yourself is most likely related to a network of beliefs that you took on or created at an earlier time in your life.

Begin to notice the triggers that elicit physical stress symptoms. Once you notice these triggers, you will be able to set up a game plan to deal with these when they come up again. Utilize the four keys that we discussed in *Chapter One* to help you prepare for dealing with these triggers. Again, these four keys are:

A. Goal setting

B. Mental Rehearsal

C. Self-Talk

D. Arousal Control (Deep Breathing).

Beliefs Connected to Your Negative Self-Talk Messages

39. Write out one negative self-talk phrase that feels like a constant companion or an old friend.

40. Write in a stream-of-consciousness style the memories that are connected to these words. Access the earliest memory possible that is connected to these words.

41. Write out a couple of memories of times where you have successfully handled challenging and stressful situations. Now write out one of the empowering

phrases you have said to yourself when you have successfully dealt with a problem.

I recently had an episode of uninvited ants invading my kitchen. At first my thoughts were connected with feelings of despair, until I asked myself the question, "What have I said to myself when I have been faced with a challenge that I was able to overcome?" The first thoughts that came to mind were the words, "You can handle this. You are bigger than this situation. Just get out your can of Raid and then tape up any possible openings where they are entering your kitchen."

My editor tells about the time that the motor of a window fan in his apartment started to catch fire from an electrical short. Rather than panicking, he simply and straightforwardly unplugged the fan, grabbed a small fire extinguisher, and put out the flames.

Update your belief system: Take a blank piece of paper and draw a vertical line down the middle of the paper. At the top of the left hand column write the word "Then" and on the right hand side write the word "Now." It is helpful to distinguish, "That was then and this is now."

8. Reframing the Situation to Create More Empowering Beliefs

When you find yourself in a stressful situation, it is important to notice what meaning you are giving to it. Are you telling yourself that this is an impossible situation? If this is true, notice if there is another meaning you can give it. Is there something you can learn from the situation? Or is there another way of minimizing the event, so you can make it a more manageable situation? Can you think about how successfully meeting this current challenge will help you feel and be stronger? When you harness the energy that was keeping the stress, doubt, and fear in place, you will be able to convert the energy into an added sense of confidence, competence, and stability.

Recently a good friend named Karen called me up because she was panicking over some erroneous information a realtor had given her about one of her out-of-state properties. My friend was feeling stressed because she was also getting ready to go on a month-long trip to Australia in less than a week and the last thing she wanted to hear was that the well on her investment property was improperly constructed.

One Friday when she called me up in a breathless panic over this revelation, I asked her to take a deep breath and create a doable action plan. We reframed the situation by helping her remember that up to this point she had successfully met every challenge that had come her way in the past fifty-some years of her life. (It is also helpful to remember that whatever words are said to people when they are in an emotionally scrambled and charged state of mind, will sink deeply into their subconscious.)

By Monday, Karen was calling me up to tell me that she had successfully resolved the situation by double-checking with other professionals in the area.

Through Story Telling, Add the Additional Empowering Frames

This brings us to the point of remembering to add empowering scenes to the stories that we are replaying in our minds. (Human beings have a habit of replaying ideas through their minds.) When the stories have endings of failure or even disaster, it is helpful to add scenes of being resourceful, even if you are not exactly sure how that looks, feels, or sounds. Start with whatever connects with your sense of being resourceful and infuse these feelings, sounds, and/or images into the new completion scene.

Find the beliefs that are embedded in each scene. Notice if these beliefs elicit a sense of being worthy, connected, hopeful, resourceful, and optimistic.

Sometimes it is helpful to add a scene that symbolizes a bridge and transition between where you are and where you are going.

When I worked with a lady in my course who was facing the idea of declaring bankruptcy, I had her imagine a three-part story. Act One took place before the bankruptcy situation, and the news of the current challenge. Act Two was about experiencing the stress and mulling over all the options. Act Three was about seeing the potential bankruptcy situation as an opportunity to rise to the occasion and to open up to new empowering ways of living. By stepping into each of these scenes, the student was able to acquire a six month, $70,000 dollar project-manager contract that she was able to do mostly from her home on a part-time basis, thereby avoiding bankruptcy.

The following paragraphs are part of the transcript with this student, named Gloria:

Gloria: Just this morning I found out that I got a contract.

Terry: Yay!

Gloria: I am managing an IT project, which I haven't done in ten years. It's going to be $70,000 dollars over the next six months for part-time work. And I can work from my home.

Terry: From your home?

Gloria: Yeah.

Terry: Awesome.

Gloria: It's kind of everything we needed. I remember exactly when this happened. I am still kind of flabbergasted.

Terry: I'm not, because you started holding a new outcome for yourself.

Gloria: Yeah. I did. [Laughter] I'm really excited. I'm still flabbergasted and kind of a little terrified to be a project manager. But OK, let's go for it. I'm gonna figure it out. So here we are.

Terry: So do you agree that God doesn't give us more than we can handle?

Gloria: Yeah.

Terry: So just to go briefly over this and we will go over it more. And I really had you in mind, Gloria, with this, although it is for all of us.

Story Process

Let us look further at the story process. We have a beginning, which is like an Act One. And in the beginning, there is usually challenge. In a screenplay, in Act One, the main character is going along with his or her life, and then there is a challenge. And the character either lies down and dies – which none of us are going to do, thankfully. So, let's have the main character say, "OK, I'll take on the challenge."

So then we are into Act Two. There are usually two parts to Act Two, but in the context here, Act Two is in one part. In Act Two, the main character is trying all sorts of ways to overcome the challenge.

What happens with our negative thoughts is that it contains a negative ending that we keep replaying. We may be asking ourselves, "Why did it happen this way instead of another way?"

What we do with this story empowerment process is that we add a new loop. We add a new ending to our internal thinking and dialogue.

Personal Story

Terry: I'll tell you a quick personal story I mentioned earlier [see *Chapter Two*) relating to this process. Many years ago I went through a separation and divorce. And it took me a really long time to complete my divorce. And I couldn't figure out why it was taking me so long. So I said, "OK, let's take a look at this."

When I was in the beginning of it, I was more in victim language – "Oh, it's happening to me." And the truth was that there was a big part of me, a BIG part of me that was ready to be divorced. But there was another part of me going, "Oh no, what am I going to do?" So I kind of reluctantly was in the middle – "How am I going to do this?" And what was happening to me was that I kept visualizing an ending that was terrible and I couldn't figure out what was going on.

And I did a process, which we will demonstrate in my next round of classes, where I found out that I was identifying with my grandmothers. When they lost their partner, they never had another partner. That part of their lives was over. Once I could see that, I went into the new ending. And since then, lots of interesting things have happened. So once I was able to visualize a new ending and to say to myself, "I am not my either of my grandmothers. I live in very different times. My parents were not from the old country like my grandparents. And I can rework my beliefs."

That's why I am teaching this – because it has been a fascinating process. So then I could create a more positive ending. And as soon as I created the ending, I finished the divorce within ten days. And I went to shake my ex-husband's hand and he gave me a hug. He was probably really glad to have it over. But, for me, I really needed to put on that new ending. And I think what happens when we get stuck in negative loops is that we are giving our stories endings that are not satisfying.

Have you ever walked out of a movie and felt terrible that it didn't end in the way that you wanted it to end? It's kind of like that with our internal stories.

Myra: Why do you think you were identifying with your grandmothers?

Terry: Because I loved them, and they were role models for me. They were really strong, vibrant women. One grandmother knew seven languages and was a doctor and came from Russia to Switzerland where she got her degree and was married for over fifty years to my grandfather. She had a lot of love for me and she gave me sage advice. And my other grandmother was very resilient. She pulled her family out of the Depression by becoming an accountant. And also I spent more time with them than with my mother, who was a professional. Does that answer your question?

But the thing is, what is really important, is that I did not have the knowledge that it was an unconscious belief that was holding me back from finishing my divorce. All I knew was that there was some reason why I didn't want to let go. So I had to uncover what was holding me back.

Myra: We sort of hang on to what is familiar.

Terry: Yes. We hang on to what is familiar. Also, if we have seen one story unfold and we didn't like that ending, we are going to do what we can to not repeat that same ending.

Myra: Consciously, but unconsciously we hang onto what is hardwired.

Terry: Yes, that's true. So this course is about finding the hardwired beliefs and structures too. Recapitulation helps us deflate these beliefs that are held up with energy and to dissolve the structures on one level and so we can also find out consciously what those structures were.

Did you want to share or check in more, Myra?

Thank you. Gloria, is there anything else you would like to share?

Gloria: I finally have my voice to sing again.

Terry: Yeah.

Gloria: I do feel like I don't want to take total credit for what is happening. Just two nights ago I was telling Jonathon, "You know, we have two months of reserves left and then we are moving to Texas to live with your mother." You know this was like two nights ago.

Terry: Right!

Gloria: I was telling him that and you know I really feel like I have been vacillating between panic and feeling like this is not going to happen this way.

Terry: Right.

Gloria: This is not going to happen this way.

Terry: So it's like a seesaw, right?

Gloria: Yeah. I think there have just been these turning points that I have come to in the process of going to the class. I went to a bankruptcy attorney several weeks ago and I came to the class that night. And after the bankruptcy attorney, after we left, I said to Jonathon, "We are not going to declare bankruptcy!"

Terry: So you gave yourself a powerful sentence. You didn't just feel it, you proclaimed it. We have been working a lot on sentences and how they are really like magic formulas that recreate our experiences for us. And what did you want to get out of tonight?

Gloria: I would like to continue to work on my focus of positive direction. I am declaring we are not going to declare bankruptcy.

Terry: Wonderful. Congratulations on that. So you are working on a positive direction. What does that symbolize to you? How would you know that you are in a positive direction? If you were to come up here for a second, if you are game . . . [Gloria comes up on the stage.] So where is the non-positive direction in relationship to your body?

Gloria: I feel like it is behind me.

Terry: OK. And where is the positive direction?

Gloria: It's in front of me.

Terry: It is in front of you. OK, wonderful. This is a great demonstration. What I would like you to do is to take what is behind you, and bring it forward. Now why would I have her do this? So she can walk in it some more? No. So she can see it. Now put it over to one side. The reason is, if it's behind you, you can't see it. You're going, "What's back there?" So you want to be able to see it and have it in view and then know that you are moving in the direction that you want to be going. And it may be a balancing act for a while, like a seesaw. While you are noticing what is happening, you can even just imagine that it is right out in front of you. Put your hand out to the left where it might be and the right hand where the positive might be.

Imagine that it is right out in front of you. Now just see the image of this limiting, negative direction, scary direction, frustrating direction, whatever you want to call it, shrink in size. Shrink it, shrink it, shrink it. Call the energy back from it. It is pure energy that is keeping it in place. Let go of whatever put it in place. Blow out whatever put it in place. Cut the chords to it. This is another form of recapitulation. Now send the good energy that you brought back in a good filtered way to this new reality that you are creating and then bring this new reality right in your front and let it expand outward. This is a form of recapitulation. OK, thank you for being willing to do this.

What was up when your eyes went up like that? That's exactly what I would like you to be aware of this week because that is where some unconscious thoughts are connected. If your unconscious could tell you what that meant right now, what would that be?

Gloria: Oh yeah, God is my source.

Terry: OK, so now let's also do the shadow part of this gesture. So what else could this gesture of raising your eyebrows while looking upward towards the ceiling mean? Does it mean, "I can't get it"?

Gloria: Holy crap! You know, is it really going to work?

Terry: So there might be something in the limbic center that you want to be able to quiet down. Just notice that.

Gloria: That it's fight, flight, or freeze?

Terry: Yeah.

Gloria: I haven't had a panic attack in a little while.

Terry: Good. What is a panic attack for you? (mirroring her gestures).

Gloria: Shaking, actually shaking. My body actually shakes and I hyperventilate and all that.

Terry: So do you have some new tools now for that not to happen?

Gloria: Yeah, the breathing. I almost had a panic attack the other night. And I just started to breathe and I could feel myself starting to hyperventilate. You know if I put my hand here (she places her hands on her solar plexus), and I don't breathe from up here and I breathe here and I feel my core. It really does send those messages to my brain to calm my body down. Thank you.

Terry: So how was that – to see that in other people, to understand that? This is what I am talking about by being able to access, until now, what has been hidden.

Reframing to Include the Hedva Steps

When people have worked with me to help them to heal their devastating experiences of betrayal, I often suggest that they read the book *Betrayal, Trust, and Forgiveness* by Beth Hedva, Ph.D. (see *Works Cited*). This author has suggested that betrayal was an experience utilized by the ancient mystery schools to train their initiates. Beth delineates five steps in the healing process of going from betrayal to renewed trust. They are as follows:

- Separation
- Purification
- Symbolic Death
- New Knowledge
- Rebirth

By examining these steps, my clients begin to reframe and transform their experience of being betrayed into an initiation experience of evolutionary growth for their soul, psyche, character, mind, emotions, and heart-wisdom. Dr. Hedva writes that all betrayal is in a sense a separation from the creator.

9. Beliefs about Happiness

Terry: This society is comprised of a lot of people who feel a lot of bio-survival anxiety. So, it is really good that you are learning these tools and realizing you have the internal resources to just manage it any time – notice it and then make a new choice. Who decides when you are happy?

Janice: I do.

Terry: Good. How much of the time do you decide it?

Janice: Not a lot.

"I'll Be Happy When..." Beliefs and the Empowering Process

Terry: OK. So I would like you to play a game. It's an important linguistic game. Have you ever heard people say, "I'll be happy when..."?

"I'll be happy when I have a computer." How long did that last? Other things came up too. So I want you to turn to someone and say when you will be happy. Pick a partner and tell them when you will be happy. [Pause.] Has everybody said when he or she will be happy?

So, I want you to go another step with this. When you say, "I'll be happy when..." I want your partner who is listening to you to then ask you the following question, "In order to do, experience and feel or be what?"

Person A is going to ask Person B the next question after the Person B has said when they will be happy.

I will demonstrate this with Bret. First he will ask me the question, "When will you be happy?"

Then he will ask me the question, "In order to do, feel, experience and/or be what?"

He will continue asking me, "In order to do, feel, experience and/or be what?"

Bret: "When will you be happy?"

Terry: When I really do know how to put my own clips in and make my own DVDs and burn them.

Bret: In order to do, feel, experience, feel and/or be what?

Terry: To be more secure in my abilities.

Bret: In order to do, feel, experience, feel and/or be what?

Terry: To feel more confident.

Bret: In order to do, feel, experience, and/or be what?

Terry: To feel I'm OK.

Bret: In order to do, feel, experience, and/or be what?

Terry: To know everything is perfect as it can be for me. To feel peace. [Pause.] Thank you. So, that's why I want you to do using the "I'll be happy if, when, or what" exercise.

Take a few minutes and go through this exercise with another person or in your journal or workbook. Notice when you are unconsciously choosing unhappiness/disagreement with what is currently happening in your life. Thank the situation and then make a new conscious choice to be happy in the moment.

By choosing acceptance and happiness with what is true in this very moment, you will have more energy, be proactive, and choose what you really want to experience in your life. This is an empowering process of consciously choosing to be happy in this moment because you are harnessing the energy that had been formerly tied up in your resistance tactics and applying this new found energy to proactive choices will give you more of what you want and less of what you don't want.

10. PV to BV, Symbols and Beliefs.

Present View of Your Situation to Better View of Your Situation

We introduced this concept/technique previously in *Chapter One*, in regard to goal setting and mental rehearsal. Here we look at it again, in regard to symbols and beliefs.

Images and symbols connect with the right hemisphere of people's brains. Take a blank sheet of paper and draw a vertical line down the center of the page. At the bottom of the left side write "PV" (Present Life View) to "BV" (Better Life View).

On the left side of the paper, draw a stick figure representation of the key elements of your present life. Notice the beliefs are connected to this present life representation.

On the right side draw a stick figure representation of the future life that you want to manifest. Imagine what beliefs you think are attached to this future life.

What is in the gap between your present life view and your better life view? Close your eyes and imagine yourself journeying from the present view to the future view. Are you walking over a bridge, sailing a boat, driving a car, or taking a plane from one location to the other? If so imagine what image would symbolize a successful completion of this journey from one side to the other. Draw this symbol or find an image on the computer or in a magazine and place it in the middle of the page. Now post this PV to BV in a location where you can see it daily. Perhaps you want to attach it to your refrigerator, bathroom mirror, or computer frame.

11. Beliefs, Jesus, and Healing

Another significant author and teacher included in my evolutionary growth process is Robert Dilts, who wrote the book *Beliefs, Pathways to Healing & Well-Being*. [p.1-2.). When his mother was dying of cancer, he made a decision to take several weeks to help her discover her limiting beliefs that were contributing to her debilitated condition. After working with her on her beliefs and lifestyle choices, she elected to not have surgery and she lived another fifteen years. In fact, she also became an internationally recognized speaker and role model.

Robert Dilts talks about the way Jesus healed. Healing has to do with the words "I-am-I" which has to do with curing or repairing and healing and therapy. He was able to address people's limiting beliefs. And He was able to engage them in such a way that He was able to bypass their conscious mind and really help them come into a place of healing. He was able to help them begin to feel hopeful when they felt hopeless. Where they felt helpless He found a way to help them feel capable and responsible. And where they felt worthless He helped them feel worthy and have a sense of belonging.

So the Bible is full of the beliefs that were connected with Him. Remember he said:

Jesus told them, "I tell you the truth. If you had faith even as small as a mustard seed, you could say to this mountain, 'Move from here to there,' and it would move. Nothing would be impossible." *Luke 17:6*

He presented another parable to them, saying, "The kingdom of heaven is like a mustard seed, which a man took and sowed in his field." *Matthew 13:31*

"Be not afraid, only believe." *Mark 5:36*

"If thou canst believe, all things are possible to him that believeth." *Mark 9:24*

"For verily I say unto you, That whosoever shall say unto this mountain, Be thou removed, and be thou cast into the sea; and shall not doubt in his heart, but shall believe that those things which he saith shall come to pass; he shall have whatsoever he saith. Therefore I say unto you, What things soever ye desire, when ye pray, believe that ye receive them, and ye shall have them." *Mark 11:23-24*

Recognize the beliefs and how He opened up people's psyches to realize that more was possible than what they had experienced.

Your experiences will reflect your internal beliefs. We went through how we delete, generalize, and distort based on our beliefs. So, what we are focusing on is what will determine how we think about and talk about our experiences. Does that make sense?

Jesus was a master in working with beliefs and helping people to work through their limitations to come into a place of healing and completeness.

Jesus and Masterful Healers are able to help people go from:

1. Feeling helpless to feeling helped.

2. Feeling hopeless to feeling hopeful.

3. Feeling worthless to feeling worthy.

Remember: You are a magnificent, valuable human being!

12. Exercises

Try out the following exercises to gain more confirmation of your worthiness:

Transform Beliefs related to Stress

4. Record a recent stressful situation and write out what physical symptoms you experienced and what negative self-talk you were replaying in your mind.

5. Write out what beliefs are attached to these negative self-talk messages.

6. Have compassion for yourself!

7. Write out new empowering beliefs.

8. Assign new meaning to formerly disempowering situations.

9. Journal about a situation that still triggers painful feelings. Then explore what filters you have been employing to keep this painful situation in place.

10. Notice what you have been deleting, distorting, and generalizing about the situation.

11. Write out a new, more empowering perspective on this situation by deconstructing and eliminating the generalization words such as "never" or "always" from your explanation of the situation. This will help you understand where you have also been employing the filters of distortion and deletion.

12. Take a situation that up to this point has not been successfully resolved and go through the Wolinsky Identity Questions that are listed earlier in this chapter.

13. Take an unsatisfying personal story that you have been replaying in your mind and add a new ending to it.

14. Practice including this new ending every time your mind replays this story.

15. Notice the new feelings that are evoked with the new ending in place.

16. Take time to record whatever positive changes happen in your life as a result of adding this new ending to your old story.

17. Create a page of Present View (PV) and future Better View (BV) drawings of your situation. Post it in a place where you will be able to see it on a daily basis.

18. Journal any changes that happen as a result of this exercise.

19. Notice if this exercise transforms some of your formerly limiting beliefs.

20. Do the "I'll Be Happy When....." exercise with a friend. Ask your friend the following questions: "When will you be happy?" and after they answer, ask "In order to do, experience and/or feel what?" Repeat this second question until your friend gets to the most core level feeling answer possible. It may take 4-8 times of asking this second question. Then reverse roles.

Chapter Three: Enlightenment about Emotions

1. Introduction

The intention of this chapter is to show how to become emotionally literate by developing skills to modulate your moods. This chapter will help you to:

- Understand the physiology and significance of your emotions. Each emotion highlights the significance of the moment.

- Embrace your emotions by changing your breathing to deep belly breathing, calming your fight/flight/flee responses when appropriate, and acting on them when necessary.

- Dissolve your judgments about having emotions.

- Decipher the messages of your emotions.

- Develop empowering feelings by putting your emotions and feelings in a positive context.

- Give voice to the meaning of your emotions and feelings.

- Be proactive by being compassionate with yourself and making life-affirming, growth-oriented decisions that lead to healthful, smart lifestyle choices.

2. Sex and Emotions

My Personal Story

Although our first emotional experiences of infancy and childhood are not exactly related to sex, our first young adult emotional experiences do tend to be. If you ask most people about their first romantic/sexual encounter, most people will immediately connect with vivid memories and thoughts about that time in their life.

In my own case, I encountered the absolute exhilaration of the fulfillment of my teenage yearnings and the depths of despair related to the rage with which my father reacted to my beautiful awakening.

During the summer of my fifteenth year, while recovering from minor surgery, I stayed with my grandmother at the Jersey shore instead of going away to camp (as I had done every summer since age nine). There I fell in love with a college freshman. Understandably, my parents were not prepared for my sexual awakening. Rather than sit down and talk with me about this significant time in my life, my father took me for a walk on the boardwalk and proceeded to angrily called me hurtful names and threaten to convict my boyfriend of statutory rape if I ever saw him again. He then devised a plan to send me to Vermont for three weeks to be with my brother, who was working as a cook at a camp that followed Native American ways.

This intense experience of going from extreme bliss to extreme emotional pain motivated me to learn how to help other men and women who have experienced trauma related to their growing up and their sexuality. In fact, this experience led me to devote eleven years to assisting Margot Anand, internationally acclaimed authority on tantra (and founder of Sky Dancing Tantra) (*margotanand.com*), with her weeklong workshops in tantra.

In these workshops, I repeatedly witnessed how the more intimate tantric processes caused deep-seated emotional pain to flare up in people. This motivated me to focus on finding ways to help people when current situations in their lives triggered an emotional breakdown. Later, while in a writing class, I wrote the following semi-fictionalized fragment about my experiences as an assistant to tantra workshop participants who were experiencing an intimate and intense session, which illustrates some of the depth of emotions that can be stirred during tantra.

Elsie and Greg and Tantra

Greg [not his real name] signaled me to attend to his partner, Elsie, who lay sprawled on the mat. Her naked body trembled as uncontrollable tears streamed over her reddened cheeks. In between her semi-conscious gasps for breaths, she muttered, "I can't find the love. I can't feel the love."

Beads of sweat amassed on Greg's forehead as his eyes conveyed desperately, "What do I do now?" He lay his naked body beside Elsie's, stroking and caressing her dampened hair.

Hoping not to disturb the rest of the group, I knelt down beside them and whispered into Elsie's ear, "It's alright. You are loved. You are loveable." These were the instinctive words that came forth from my lips.

Elsie kept shivering and saying, "I can't find the love. I can't feel ANYTHING." Not knowing what to do, and flying by the seat of my pants, so to speak, I uttered a barely audible prayer to God while raising my left hand to act as antenna/conduit to God's loving energy, while gliding my right hand about an inch above her body, over her heart area, hopefully channeling divine energy to her.

"Take some deep breaths and know that you are loved. You are loveable. You are love," I uttered. These were the only words that came to my mind. As God, Greg, and I continued to hold her in a circle of compassion, her tears slowed, and her breaths deepened until she fell into a deep sleep. We then placed a sheet over her and left her to regenerate in the womb of the sacred circle formed by the workshop participants surrounding us.

Healing Emotional Trauma

Since the time of that experience, I have given a lot of thought to the best ways to help people when they are in an emotional breakdown. What I have found over the years of healing work, workshop facilitation, and extensive research is that the most important methods of helping people involve the following steps:

21. Realize that, most likely, the emotional upset they are experiencing in the moment signifies that they are in an age-regressed state to the time when the related emotional trauma originally occurred.

22. Rather than trying to minimize their pain in order to help them feel better, acknowledge the magnitude of their pain.

23. Ask them if it is all right to touch them on their shoulders, arm, lower back or belly. (Some people will say yes, while others will not want to be touched at all). There are also acupressure points (such as P6, just above the wrist on the inside of the arm) that can be very calming to the person.

24. Notice your own breathing, and take deep breaths, so that the person in breakdown can feel your sense of calm, centeredness, and support.

25. Then ask the person to start taking deeper breaths. This will help them begin to calm their limbic system.

26. Notice what they are saying about themselves in this state. For instance, if they were told that they were "no good", "worthless", etc., reassure them that you do notice their value and goodness.

27. Realize that what you say to the person who is in emotional breakdown will penetrate into their subconscious and assist their healing process.

This can also be a beneficial practice for you: If you are in an intensified state, choose proactive directives to think in your mind such as, "I can and will get through this successfully," because the same idea holds true for you. Whatever you think and say to yourself (and out loud) will settle into your unconscious. These thoughts will become part of your unconscious operating system.

Upon further reflection, I have realized that my drive to work in tantra communities was due to the fact that my unconscious was still seeking to heal my original trauma of the loss of my father's love related to my own sexual awakening.

The irony of my father and mother's angry and extreme reaction was that their action had an "out-of-the-frying-pan-into-the-fire" effect, because the camp where my brother worked was a remote one where all the boys and men wore either loincloths or nothing at all. (However, because I was under my brother's guardianship, none of the males dared to touch or disrespect me in any way.) In any event, when as an adult I chose to work in the tantra community (as a teacher and assistant on the staff of Margo Anand), I was comfortable around naked men and had an expectation that I would not be disrespected in any way.

According to a well-known Chicago male therapist and seminar trainer, most men have only two feelings: anger and sexual feelings. (Another simplistic variation on this idea is the joke (*www.smilespedia.com/top-100-funniest-one-*

liners-on-the-internet), "Men have two emotions: Hungry and Horny. If you see him without an erection, give him a sandwich." When I was privy to the men's private meetings during the three weeks that I stayed at the Indian camp, I experienced men expressing the gamut of emotions including tears and grief over deep losses in their lives. But, still, in my own experience, it HAS been easier to enroll men in seminars where sex is discussed versus where emotions are discussed.

In fact one saying that made its way around several circles of another relationship-oriented organization was the riddle: "Emotions are to women, what ___ are to men." The answer: "opinions". In other words, women feel accepted and appreciated when their emotions are heard and respected, whereas men feel accepted and appreciated when their opinions are heard and respected.

Another curious idea that was put forth by another seminar leader was the saying that: "Men often yell, when they are really sad, and women often cry when they are really angry."

Perhaps, particular incidents and people come to mind when you read the above statement. Whether or not this is always true, it is reasonable to say that, at this point, our emotions are still not well understood by most people.

In fact, when I was thinking about writing this chapter, I would muse over the idea about what I would say if an interviewer asked me, "What about emotions?" My answer would go along these lines: "Yeah, I've got some. How about you?"

For the most part, our society up to this point in time has not set aside the time and funding to thoroughly educate people on the meaning of their emotions, how to access them, define them, redefine them when necessary, and resolve them and on how to utilize the energy that they have had tied up in limiting emotions. If they did this, we would move toward creating smarter, happier, more productive, and healthier people. Some educators are beginning to address that many of their students' learning disabilities are related to emotional unrest in the home environment.

3. Feelings and Emotions

In this chapter, we are exploring the physiological and psychological aspects of emotions. We will also examine specific ways to access and resolve painful past emotions and emotional memories. We will also look at the way our brains and bodies store long-term and short-term memories, which means that we will acknowledge the body-mind connections that exist in all human beings. We will briefly explore the differences in the way men's and women's brains process emotions and emotional memories. Finally, we will also study the origin, effects, and healing of emotional trauma.

Although it is not meant to be a definitive scientific or psychological thesis on the various dimensions of emotions, this chapter is designed to stir your curiosity and motivate you to do your own research and work in understanding the ways emotions impact your life and the lives of your loved ones, friends, co-workers, and communities.

According to Louis H. du Preez, Ph.D., who is an EQ (emotional intelligence, cf., IQ) organizational consultant and a senior lecturer at Potchefstraoom University in South Africa, "A feeling is the response part of the emotion. Emotion is an 'umbrella term' which includes the situation, the interpretation/perception of the situation and the response or feeling related to the perception of the situation." (Google Answers *answers.google.com/answers/main?cmd=threadview&id=149261*).

In other words (according to Eric Jensen, Ph.D. author of *The Learning Brain*), emotions are: "Biologically driven, cross-cultural responses to environmental stimuli." Jensen states that the difference between emotions and feelings are: "Emotions are cross cultural – the same all over the world. Feelings are a subset of all of our mind-body states (disappointment, hunger, hope, etc. There are hundreds of them!). Feelings are a learned response appropriate to the culture in which you grow up (family, peers, community, etc.)"

(*Google Answers answers.google.com/answers/main?cmd= threadview&id=149261*).

Emotional responses for the most part are generated unconsciously. These responses alert us to potential impacts on our physical, emotional and psychological well-being from aspects of our environment and relationships. These impacts may be positive and life-enhancing or threatening.

4. The Physiology of Emotions

According to Joseph LeDoux, author of *The Emotional Brain*, emotions are "biological functions of the nervous system" and should be studied as brain functions rather than simply as psychological states (p.12).

Emotions are designed to meet our biological survival needs. So, it is common for our physiological responses to happen before we have a conscious awareness of what is going on in our environment, because the more primitive parts of our brains have been hardwired to detect minute to large changes in our environment before our prefrontal cortex has responded.

Have you ever heard people say, "I have a funny feeling about this," or "This situation makes my stomach churn"? Our biological systems are designed to keep us alive. If there is something not right in our environment, our bodies will detect it first. Perhaps you can think of expressions that signify the fine-tuning abilities of our physiology. Another phrase that comes to mind is, "This situation makes my hair stand on end."

So often in our society, we have been taught to validate our physical challenges, but not our emotional challenges. There are very few bosses that accept an employee taking a day off of work for pleasure, yet if that same employee needs a root canal, usually there is an immediate approval of their need for time off. This is just one example of the ways people have been taught to validate their physical needs (especially when there is pain attached to them), but to invalidate their emotional needs (even when there is pain attached to them).

In my opinion, we are a society that is in need of gaining greater understanding, acceptance, and appreciation of our emotions and emotional needs. According to Tian Dayton, well-known author and talk show guest (*www.tiandayton.com*), the definition of emotional health includes emotional literacy and the ability to modulate our emotions (Dayton, *Trauma and Addiction* p.42). But in order to gain the ability to modulate our emotions, we need to gain the ability to *accept our emotions*, rather than judge them. We also need to be able to give voice to these emotions and give empowering meaning and context to the emotions as they are occurring.

One of the reasons that our society has not been as accepting of the need to understand emotions is because the emotional wiring varies between men and women. It has been scientifically proven that women have larger emotional processing centers in their brains, including a larger hippocampus.

Joseph LeDoux's book, *The Emotional Brain*, emphasizes the importance of understanding how our bodies and minds experience and process emotions. He asserts that our brains have separate pathways for emotions related to fear versus emotions related to procreation and pleasure.

Another way to state this is through understanding the common denominators regarding emotional responses:

- All emotions are related to our innate and unconscious response to survive. Because our brains are hardwired for survival, our emotional responses, which are unconscious physiological responses, are generated in the more primitive part of the brain (the limbic brain).

- These unconscious responses override our logical responses, which are generated in our brain's prefrontal cortex.

Thus, people tend to judge and minimize their emotional responses as "wrong" because they are often out of their conscious control. Yet, if we are able to embrace our emotions as unconscious responses that are wired into our central nervous systems to help us keep our bodies safe (or to experience pleasure), then we are able to find the important information hidden in our emotions and take appropriate action.

When your body tenses up in a fight, flight, or freeze response, thank your body for informing you that danger is at hand. Or if you are experiencing a heightened response by your senses, enjoy the moment and make wise decisions to help you sustain the pleasure through more than a fleeting moment of time.

Next time you feel "butterflies" in your stomach, goose bumps on your skin, or a feeling of repulsion when you smell food that has spoiled, thank your body for informing you that you are experiencing an event that holds some form of significance for you and take appropriate action. When you feel the butterflies, acknowledge that your body is communicating to you the importance of this current event; or if you are feeling goose bumps, embrace the possible unique pleasure of the moment, or if your face and body are cringing over the smell of rotten food, throw out the food and find something fresher and more nourishing for your body, mind, and emotions.

Breathe into them

Give words to your feelings,

Create new empowered meaning

for these emotions and feelings.

Then make proactive decisions.

5. Touch and Emotions

Our body's largest organ is our skin. In an average-sized man it weighs about eight pounds and has an area of about nineteen square feet. Our experience with touch begins the moment we are born when a medical practitioner helps our tiny body come out of the womb and into the world. This primal experience of being held sends immediate positive survival-oriented signals to our brain. This immediate touch becomes one of our first sensations of gaining a physical and emotional sense of well-being in the physical world.

According to Dr. Clyde W. Ford in his informative book, *Compassionate Touch*, emotions are connected with touch. The following except from his book connects the experience of emotions with touch (Ford, *Compassionate Touch*, "The Birth of Emotions" p.31-32).

"Why are emotions experienced so profoundly through touching the body? One answer to this question begins even prior to birth, barely two weeks into life, at a time when the human embryo resembles a tiny plate, two millimeters long, with a groove down the middle. This plate is poised on the verge of great change. On either side of the central groove, ridges are about to push up as though a volcanic eruption were causing a new mountain range to form along a river canyon. These ridges, called the neural crest, and the valley between them, the neural groove, are part of a layer of the embryo called the ectoderm.

Neural crest cells eventually give rise to the skin and majority of the brain and nervous system. In other words, the structures that allow us to feel sensation (the skin and receptors) and the structures that allow us to experience emotions arise from the same group of cells. Feelings, as in sensation, and feeling, as in emotional experience, share a common heritage in the body...This relationship between body and emotions continues after birth." (Ford, Ibid.).

According to neurobiologists, memories are stored in various parts of the brain. Much of what goes on in the subconscious still remains a mystery.

6. Emotional Literacy

As a postscript/epilogue to the story of my sexual awakening (see the previous *Section 3*), eventually I realized that the work that needed to be done to resolve the trauma was related to Tian Dayton's emotional literacy resolution model (Dayton, *Trauma and Addiction*, p.42-47).

As I developed more effective ways to embrace my emotions, I regained my sense of authentic self, as well as my peace of mind, body and spirit.

The four stages to develop and maintain emotional literacy, (delineated by Tian Dayton in her book, *Trauma and Addiction* p.42-47) are as follows:

    28. **Feel the fullness of the emotion.** I recommend doing this by accepting all of the physical sensations

and thoughts connected with the specific emotion. The best way to do this is to:

- Acknowledge that you are having an emotional experience.

- Rather than trying to suppress the emotion, change your breathing pattern from shallow breathing to deeper belly breathing.

29. **Label it.** In other words, categorize the emotion. For instance, is it sadness, grief, anger, despair, fear, frustration, jealousy, sexual feelings, or joy? The emotional experience that is happening in the moment may be a composite of several emotions. It will benefit you to identify as many of the emotions that are present in the moment.

    When you name the emotion, you will diminish the sense of being confused and overwhelmed that is often associated with the moments when you are feeling intense experiences.

    In this society, most of us have grown up with unspoken and spoken lessons in ways to ignore, suppress, and invalidate our emotions. Think of the expressions that people utilize when they are instructing other people to override their emotions, such as, "Keep a stiff upper lip," or "Big girls (or boys) don't cry."

    Rather than continue to view emotions as a weakness and vulnerability, regard emotions as messages that are connected with your innate survival instincts.

3. **Explore the meaning and function within the self.** Each emotion has valuable messages and guidance for us. Rather than seeing any particular emotion as

an unwanted guest, look at it as a significant teacher doing its best to communicate the need to help you stay alive, vibrant, and conscious of the importance of the present moment.

4. **Choose whether or not to communicate our inner state to another person.** If you think that talking out your feelings and emotions with someone you respect and trust, who is able to acknowledge and validate your experience just as it is, will help you, then by all means communicate with this person about them.

I also employed the four stages of grief work discussed by Dr. Dayton and others (Dayton, *Trauma and Addiction*, p. 182; see also: "What Stage of the Grief and Loss Process are You in at this Point of The Recession?," by Tian Dayton, Ph.D., www.huffingtonpost.com/dr-tian-dayton/what-stage-of-the-grief-a_b_184768.html) to complete the grieving work around the loss of the emotional support and closeness with my father.

Also see *Chapter Six* on recapitulation later in this book for some very powerful approaches to overcoming grief.

Chapter Four:
All about Transformation

"Transformation requires the willingness to challenge your basic beliefs about who you are. We must have the faith to trust responses and sensations that we can't fully understand, and a willingness to experience ourselves flowing in harmony with the primitive, natural laws that will take over and balance our seemingly incongruous perceptions. Traumatized people must let go of all kinds of beliefs and preconceptions in order to complete the journey back to health."

– Peter A. Levine, *Waking the Tiger* (p. 204)

Have you ever wondered why it is so difficult to make certain changes in your life? Perhaps you want to change your weight, your job, or your relationship. Or perhaps you want to increase your physical health and vitality. Have you ever made New Year's resolutions that you fail to keep within a week of making them?

If so, this chapter is for you because we will explore the various elements that help you create the transformation you have been aiming to achieve. We will also address what you need to do to maintain the transformation you have worked so hard to achieve.

1. The B.E.S.T. System

B.E.S.T. is the acronym for understanding the importance of:

- **B:** Beliefs
- **E:** Emotional literacy – mood management
- **S:** Support systems for effective reinforcement
- **T:** Trusting your instinct, inner wisdom, and guidance.

***Breathe and Believe It Is Possible –
and Rework Your Beliefs!***

Beliefs

Chapter Two was dedicated to exploring the structure, nature, and significance of beliefs. So it is sufficient here to cite again the Merriam-Webster online dictionary definition of beliefs, which is: "a state or habit of mind in which trust or confidence is placed in some person or thing."

When we explore the nature and structure of beliefs, we are then able to learn ways to deconstruct the belief and create a series of beliefs that help us obtain the transformation we are committed to obtaining and maintaining.

Embrace emotional literacy

Review chapter three. Understanding the true context and meaning of your emotions will help you to become more effective in carrying forth your action plan to transform your life. Why? Because emotions sometimes block you from feeling and being the best you possibly can. Up until now, emotional literacy has not been well understood by most people. Instead, most people have been taught to numb out and invalidate their feelings. If, on the other hand, you are willing to utilize your emotions to help you feel empowered, you will have a better chance of feeling energized, vital and confident in carrying forth your commitment to fully evolve your life and live the best life possible.

Sustain your progress by maintaining effective support systems.

This brings us to the next key feature of the B.E.S.T. system. Obtaining mentors that model what you wish to achieve is a necessary step in creating your best life, because it helps your psyche understand that what you aspire to do is possible! When you look at these mentors you will also find that they have set up support systems that help them obtain their desired dreams and goals.

We are communal beings by nature. Feeling the strength of a group of people that are rooting for you will help you feel empowered.

Trust your true self and your soul's purpose.

Living your authentic self involves being able to accept, acknowledge and trust your instincts and internal guidance. Many people get bogged down with limited feelings and beliefs of: helplessness, hopelessness, and feelings of unworthiness. Many of these feelings are related to limiting imprints imparted by your original caregivers – your parents and other caregivers and early authority figures.

Have you heard the saying, "He's a chip off the old block"? Taking on these negative imprints is a natural survival mechanism for all human beings.

So, now that we have briefly summarized the key aspects of the BEST system, let us examine the elements of "Transformation".

2. Transformation Defined

So what exactly is transformation? And if it's a good thing, how do you get it and keep it? According to the online Merriam-Webster dictionary, some of the definitions of the word "transform" include the following:

>*a* : to change in composition or structure
>
>*b* : to change the outward form or appearance of
>
>*c* : to change in character or condition : convert.

The word "convert" is defined by the Merriam-Webster online dictionary, (*www.merriam-webster.com/dictionary/convert*), as follows:

transitive verb

>*1a*: to bring over from one belief, view, or party to another.
>
>*1b*: to bring about a religious conversion in.
>
>*2a*: to alter the physical or chemical nature or properties of especially in manufacturing.
>
>*2b(1)*: to change from one form or function to another.
>
>*2b(2)*: to alter for more effective utilization."

3. The Power of Dissatisfaction!

These above definitions lead me to the principle that I teach called: "The Power of Dissatisfaction". When a person experiences a lack of satisfaction, they have a choice of:

1. Tolerating the dissatisfaction,

2. Repressing it until it becomes unbearable, OR

3. Utilizing the messages encoded in the feelings and choosing to be proactive.

I have found in my own life that when I remove my natural judgment about having negative feelings, I am then able to harness the energy that was trapped in the feelings of dissatisfaction and apply the energy towards more effective thoughts, choices, and actions.

If you are willing to embrace the idea that everything is made up of energy – including objects, thoughts, and actions – then you can start to direct the same energy that you are channeling into your present thoughts and actions into more satisfying and productive ones.

Sometimes, the first step is to acknowledge that you are dissatisfied, and that you can do something about it! The energy of dissatisfaction usually involves elements of feeling helpless, hopeless, fatigued, and/or worthless. Acknowledging these feelings of powerlessness unleashes your energy that was formerly tied up in resistance to your dissatisfaction.

Most people have been taught to repress their less than "pleasant/happy" feelings until they erupt in the form of rage, shame, physical distortions, and/or depression. The more a person represses these feelings, the greater sense of isolation he or she feels, which usually creates a deeper, darker downward spiral.

Depression usually includes feelings of fatigue, futility, being overwhelmed, and worthlessness. Although I don't claim to have the definitive answers on the best ways to deal with depression, I have found that some and perhaps all of the symptoms of depression can be relieved through connecting with the right support system. These systems may be in the form of medical assistance, religious affiliations, and alternative healing groups. The most important first step in my opinion is to come out of isolation and find the best support system possible.

4. Steps to Transformation

How does this relate to transformation? Is it possible to convert limiting physical and emotional experiences into healthier and happier experiences? I have found the following seven steps very effective in transforming one feeling and experience into another:

1. Acknowledge the current limiting and/or negative feeling.

2. Be compassionate with yourself and breathe into the feelings.

3. Be willing to listen to your body and the messages of what your body and mind need in the moment to help you effectively transform your limiting belief and/or feeling. For instance, if you feel tired in the middle of the afternoon, rather than judging yourself for feeling tired, listen to your body and find out what it really needs for your body to feel restored, such as a mini nap and/or vitamin (e.g., B or C) supplement.

4. Then be willing to be proactive and take action to address your current needs in the healthiest way possible.

5. Acknowledge the little steps you take because this will help you stay focused on your path of positive choices and actions. As the Kahuna (Hawaiian

shaman) saying goes, "Energy flows where attention flows!"

6. Connect with a good support system that also helps you stay focused on positive action.

7. Implement a good system that also helps you access your subconscious feelings and re-pattern them. There are several excellent hypnosis/ meditation products that will help you work with re-patterning your limiting subconscious thoughts.

In summary, in following these steps you are creating a more empowering context for each feeling and then choosing proactive actions to evolve your life in a more positive and productive direction.

5. Five Element Theory; Creation Cycle

Another interesting perspective on Transformation is presented in the Creation Cycle of the Five Element Theory of Chinese Medicine. According to the Five Element Theory, the human body is made up of the five earth elements:

- Wood
- Fire
- Earth
- Metal
- Water.

Each element has a nourishing quality and a controlling quality. For instance, Water controls Fire and is capable of extinguishing it. On the other hand, Water nourishes Wood. Each element is also related to the twelve meridians and the major organs of the body. Each organ and element is also related to specific emotions. In Chinese Medicine, the acupuncturist, herbalist, and shiatsu practitioner seek to re-establish balance in the body, emotions, mind, and spirit.

The following chart relates each of the five elements to their corresponding organs and emotions:

Element	Yin and Yang Organs	Emotion
Earth	Spleen and Stomach	Worry
Metal	Lung and Large Intestine	Grief
Water	Kidney and Bladder	Anxiety
Wood	Liver and Gallbladder	Anger
Fire	Heart and Small Intestine	Joy

In the Creation Cycle of Chinese Medicine, one element transforms into the next element in service to the human body and the elemental Earth Plane. As Wood is utilized to produce heat, the element of Fire transforms the Wood forms into heat and ash.

The form of ash is then integrated into the Earth, which also holds the roots of the trees. The Earth mixed with ash then transforms into minerals. Thus we have the element of Metal.

Metal becomes a container for Water, and Water nourishes and feeds the Wood element, and so on and so forth. So, when we speak of transformation, we embody the element of motion and adaptability.

For a human being, transformation in its most positive light reflects the quality of service. Just as Wood is in the service of Fire to produce heat, a person is in the service of people, places, things, and, most importantly, spirit.

As you expand your actions of service, you transform your perceived identities and value on this Earth Plane.

Now that we have explored transformations of forms based on service, it is also important to explore other related aspects of transformation, such as a change in identity and behaviors, and the shift in identities and corresponding patterns connected to subconscious imprinting.

6. Identity Transformations

When a person, place, or thing changes the nature of its service and context, it also takes on a new identity. A good example of this concept can be found in the stages in the dissolution of a marriage and/or the loss of a life mate/partner.

Beth Hedva delineates the stages that a person encounters when they experience a traumatic betrayal. (Hedva, *Betrayal, Trust and Forgiveness* p. 32) Also, she indicates that betrayal and loss was the first step of the initial process for mystery school initiates.

The stages are:

1. Loss-Betrayal-Separation

2. Purging-Cleansing

3. Symbolic Death

4. New Knowledge

5. Rebirth and New Identity.

When a person experiences an irrevocable loss or separation, the person goes through an identity transformation. In Beth Hedva's steps (which are not necessarily always a linear process), the initiate first experiences Loss-Betrayal-Separation, which includes loss of former identity.

The second stage, Purging-Cleansing, involves grieving, which might include tears. These tears are a cleansing process of the body, which, among other things, is a way of making room for the new.

In the third, Symbolic Death, the old reliable identities and support systems are no longer sufficient to fully serve the person's life, so the person must learn new skills, which leads to the fourth stage, New Knowledge.

This new knowledge then helps the person serve the community in a new and hopefully better way. At this point, the person begins to fully inhabit his/her new identity and new roles of service. Thus, we realize the fourth stage, Rebirth and New Identity.

In my own life, I experienced an intense identity shift when I went through the dissolution of a thirteen-year marriage. I went from being a married woman to being a divorcee. The work that I had chosen to do while I had been married no longer made sense to me when I embodied my newfound freedom. So I went from being known as a realtor to being known as a teacher, shiatsu therapist, and painter. My values shifted from a sense of serving my former partner's life and career to delving more deeply into my own interests and skill development.

Not only did the identity shifts take place on the level of thought and behavior, but my body also experienced changes connected to the changes in my relationship identities.

When a person experiences a loss (consciously chosen or not), the limbic system experiences the sense of loss and perhaps triggers survival responses of fight, flight, and/or freeze as well as possibly the female dynamic of "tend and befriend". In regard to the last, I personally found it important to join a support group of women who understood what was involved in the changes I was experiencing – emotionally, physically, psychically, and spiritually.

Internal Identity Transformations

"...The brain can change its structure and organization as it's influenced by experience." (Rosenblum, *See What I'm Saying: The Extraordinary Powers of Our Five Senses*, p. xii) Our brains respond to changes. Change itself is neither good nor bad. What makes it good or bad is the perspective and context we assign to change. One example of such change is our body's experience of new cells replacing old/dying cells.

"We are not like machines – our bodies constantly repair and renew themselves. And unlike a brand new car, which starts to wear out the moment it leaves the showroom, a newborn baby's immunity, coordination, heart and circulation will actually 'improve' during its first decade." (Rosenblum) Our bodies continually update our systems, as do our thoughts, identities, functions, and beliefs.

In the literal as well as the figurative sense, our entire beings continue the transformation process on both the micro and macro levels throughout our entire lives.

We naturally, consciously, and unconsciously change our self-perceptions throughout our entire lives. When our bodies evolve out of childhood formation into more adult formations we give ourselves new identities. Whereas we once considered ourselves children, as we grow we move into our adult identities. Society also supports these transformations and identity changes.

Our internal perceptions, images, and self-talk also correspond to the external changes that our bodies and personalities experience. We outgrow clothing, behaviors, and preferences of all sorts. What is most important here is to examine what we tell ourselves about the changes in our lives?

Our Internal Dialogues and Monologues

When we have intense experiences and interactions, we create a corresponding internal conversation script about our perceptions of the experience. Once we have established that script, we tend to replay it over and over again – especially when we encounter situations that remind us (either on a conscious or unconscious level) of the original trauma.

For many years, I felt compelled to enroll in remedial writing courses year after year until I realized that I was replaying an incomplete conversation in my head. The conversation was between me and my former college advisor named Kit, who was a wonderful writer. Kit advised me to take remedial writing courses because she felt they would serve me well for my entire life. Even though I silently agreed with her advice, my college did not offer remedial writing courses, so I muddled through my academic courses and focused on my art and music projects instead.

It was not at least two and a half decades after I received Kit's wise advice that I begin to seek out writing teachers. Even though I found phenomenal teachers and mentors, there was a part of myself that kept holding my brain back from fully integrating their lessons on grammar and composition into my writing.

Earlier this year, I was looking into *still more* remedial writing courses when I finally realized that I had never evolved and concluded the internal conversation with Kit, and it was still alive in my mind. Once I realized this, I created an internal movie script in which I thanked Kit for her guidance and let her know that I was very happy that I had finally followed through on her advice. By completing this conversation with her in my mind, I was finally able to overcome my blocks and move forward with my writing, including being able to write this book.

One of my recently departed mentors, who knew about my deep love of writing, wrote in a letter to me her heartfelt guidance which is currently taped to the bottom frame of my computer. As I related in the dedication on page two of this book, the words in her letter are as follows:

"Dear Terry: You are the only you in the whole world and universe, and you do know what you are meant to do – to express and fulfill the divine idea that was in you before you incarnated. It is a sacred and precious trust to keep. No one can give you yourself but you. You have learned and gained from others – others' 'paradigms', but if you feel and think that those in any way delay your 'thing' and your writing your book, your choice is obvious, I think. Also, assure yourself that as you establish and pursue your path, God will sustain and support you because it is GOD'S WORK. Free yourself of obligations. (I know it is not easy – but your own path is much more important). Love yourself more than ever before. Love, Marion"

Ms. Marion Dickes served as a spiritual mentor to me for almost twenty years. She was the founder and head of The World Healing Ministry located in San Diego, California. Whenever I called her on the phone she most graciously welcomed my calls and immediately began to pray for me. Just knowing that she was on my side helped me to successfully resolve whatever challenge was present in my life at the time of my request. She was a wonderful writer and also a Doctor of Divinity. Her life, work, and loving relationship continue to inspire me.

Marion always brought out the best in me by focusing on my core goodness. My memories of Marion's compassionate acceptance and guidance continue to comfort me in passing moments of doubt, insecurity, or confusion. She was another person in my life who has helped me to understand the necessity and value of maintaining good relationships with compassionate mentors in my life.

Mentors demonstrate by their physical presence what is possible to create in this life. It is difficult to maintain the changes we make, unless we can bring our subconscious thoughts into alignment with the new and desired self-image. When we connect with mentors who show us what is possible, something stirs within our own psyches. When these stirrings are harnessed into disciplined action, we too can obtain the desired results.

When I think of the word "transformation", I think of the words "trance" and "formation" because transformation usually involves integrating the thinking-feeling processes and beliefs of both the conscious and subconscious minds. To maintain our desired results, it is important to rework our internal images. These images are stored in our subconscious mind.

Jenn August's online book, *Remove Your Blocks, So Your Business Rocks* (*www.beyond-business-for-women.com*), reaffirms the importance of this phenomena in the following way:

1. Your Conscious Mind controls 20% of what you think, feel and do.

2. Your Subconscious Mind controls 80% of what you think, feel and do.

"This program is a comprehensive retraining program to reset your subconscious mind AND your conscious mind to get 100% of your mind on board with your success." Changing Internal Identity Images

I began smoking cigarettes when I was in college. By the time I moved to New York, I was totally addicted to smoking cigarettes. Even though it created a habitual smoker's cough and constant sore throat, I still would not stop smoking until one day when I just realized that smoking was no longer an enjoyable activity. At that point, rather than stopping smoking altogether (cold turkey so to speak) I gave my psyche the chance to catch up with my conscious decision. So several times a day, I would just imagine what it would be like to feel like a non-smoker again. Since this identity was stronger than my internal smoker self-image, within a few weeks, I was able to fully let go of any desire for cigarettes.

It may have helped my identity-switch practice to remember the pain my maternal grandfather suffered when his body was wracked with emphysema. My grandfather had started smoking when he was fourteen years old. He continued this practice until he became ill. By the time I was four years old, he needed to carry an oxygen tank with him. He became so sick that he died on my eighth birthday when he was in his mid-sixties.

It is clear that the process of switching internal identities often begins with you feeling discontent with your current self-identity. Therefore, it is helpful to bring to mind other people who are examples for you. Next, create a plan that includes reworking your internal self-images. Guided meditations can assist you with this process.

Another personal example of successfully altering my self-images relates to a story about the holidays. After I had ended a relationship with a life-mate, I found myself feeling sad and alone on the holidays. Rather than being a joyful celebration like the year before, when my boyfriend and I had prepared a splendid Thanksgiving dinner for twenty-five of our friends, this year the holidays felt bleak.

Fortunately I came across a wonderful meditation that I was able to utilize during my sleep. The meditation guided my subconscious to become proactive and move forward rather than dwell in the feelings of disconnection and sadness. So, the next Thanksgiving again became a time of joyful gatherings and celebrations. There was an organic sense of motivation. Internally I made a shift from feeling at the mercy of the circumstances of my life to feeling that it is possible to create satisfying situations.

We think hundreds of thousands of thoughts a day. The idea is to become the master of our thoughts. It is as if we mindlessly keep a particular radio or TV set on one channel. As the channel continues to play, we tend to ignore it with our conscious mind, while our unconscious mind continues to accept its messages. So first we must become conscious of the limiting messages that are on continual play in our minds. Then we can consciously switch the channel to thoughts that are more empowering.

Jenn August offers the following explanation for the reason this process works:

"Your brain is made up of neurons, which are tiny nerve cells that have branches that reach out to other neurons. This connection between neurons is called a neural net – in this net is where a thought or a memory is stored. If you fire a thought over and over again, it creates its own neural net and you keep it strong and healthy by thinking that thought over and over and over again. Your thoughts create a chemical response in the body.

When you interrupt a thought process, the connections that the nerve cells have to each other start to break down. You can change the chemical response in your own brain and choose to destroy old thought patterns, and you can create new thought patterns that you consciously choose and repetitively reinforce." (August, *Remove Your Blocks*, Chapter 8, p.2).

This process is similar to practicing an exercise routine that strengthens your muscles. With each training session, your muscles begin to develop greater strength and definition. This is true of practicing the conscious thought process in which your mind integrates a more empowering definition into your psyche.

As you become happier with your new self-definitions and stronger identity, your conscious mind more easily accepts the necessary practice that is required to maintain the newfound strength and definition.

Often it is necessary to have a strong motivating factor to keep your new identity and set of new behavior patterns in place. For instance, after I switched to the identity of being a non-smoker, any time I would consider becoming a smoker again, the horrendous images of remembering my grandfather dying a slow painful death would pop into my mind and keep my thoughts focused on maintaining the non-smoker identity. The internal identities of being a smoker became so innately intertwined with the horrendous images of oxygen tanks and my grandfather's cancer-ridden body that the former pleasure related to smoking never returned. Thus, I have been able to effortlessly maintain the internal and external non-smoker identity for thirty-four years.

As another example, one of the participants of my course was able to successfully switch identities from one of having the sense of being on the brink of catastrophe to one of being able to stand in a place of self-sufficiency and grace. For many people, there comes a point where there is a decision made to work through the current challenges and get to a better place. Have you ever heard the expression, "I am mad as hell and I'm not going to take it anymore!"? When a person combines a strong emotional feeling with a firm commitment, life begins to change for the better!

The emotional aspect of this decision is usually part of the subconscious response, and this link to the subconscious is a key component of the firm decision to change for the better.

When you connect with a strong emotional drive, whether it is related to anger, sadness, love, or happiness, you are more likely to follow through on your decision to change for the better. Why? The reason is that our emotions link us to our survival instincts. These survival instincts may also be related to our feelings of joy and happiness. These positive feelings usually help us feel good about being in a physical body on this Earth Plane, in spite of whatever discomforts we have to endure.

Life Decisions at Life-Death Junctures

During a Thanksgiving party, I was talking with an acquaintance who told me about his near-death experience following a serious car accident. He said that he felt the need to return to his body, rather than stay in the light. When I asked him what propelled him back into his body, he shrugged his shoulders and said, "My family – I didn't want them to be sad about me." He elaborated on his answer by saying that he didn't exactly know why he came back because he was not "close" to his family.

There are four poignant points about his story. The first is that, even though he did not feel close to his family, there was some kind of soul agreement among them to assist one another in evolving their lives – if even just by giving each person a chance to be born. It is my experience that the most painful aspects of being with my family have motivated me to heal the original pain of my childhood (that continued to play out in my adulthood) and to help others to face and heal their trauma and pain.

The second point is that every human being faces life-death junctures in their lives. The decision to remain on this

Earth Plane in one's body takes determination and usually a big shift in perspective. This shift involves placing a value on life, rather than taking it for granted.

The third point is the realization that we are not alone on this Earth Plane. There are guardian angels and God's other divine helpers watching over us to help us meet the challenges that may seem insurmountable at times.

The fourth point is that it is helpful to establish a spiritual practice that assists you in connecting with your divine guidance. Perhaps it will help to write or meditate or participate in a group that focuses on developing trust of your divinely inspired intuition and guidance.

7. Connecting Your Subconscious and Conscious Minds

Sometimes the guidance comes through our subconscious mind first. It may come in the form of a dream sequence or a physical sensation or even as a passing thought, or sometimes the divine guidance is initiated through a conscious thought and need. For instance, if you ask yourself a question and then just open to the answer presenting itself, you will usually find new ways to view the question and new ways to view the solution. Indeed, the most effective transformational work is accomplished by uniting the conscious thinking process with processes that access and evolves beliefs stored in the subconscious mind.

It is a well-known fact that Albert Einstein would take daytime naps to find solutions. Einstein's daydreaming would help him access the nonlinear, subconscious part of his brain to help him solve questions that he held in his conscious mind. To find the answers to these questions, he would go into a type of daydream/trance where his brain waves would shift from beta to alpha and theta.

There are four types of brain wave states which Einstein experienced and which you experience. They are:

1. **Beta** – the primary waking, active state for most adults and some children. It is the most externally oriented state, and is associated with the fastest brain wave frequencies, with the brain oscillating between 14 and 30 cycles per second. It is the conscious state of mind, and is associated with mental activity, focus, and anxiety, and is utilized to take and pass tests, participate in sports, or give presentations. You are alert to external stimuli and using the left hemispheres of your brain to form judgments and process information.

2. **Alpha** – related to daydreaming and meditation. You experience this state when you focus inward and disconnect from external stimuli, even just by closing your eyes. Your brain waves in this state oscillate between 8 and 13 cycles per second. It is related to the subconscious state of mind. It is a state where there is a connection between the conscious and subconscious mind (and between the left and right brain hemispheres).

3. **Theta** – an even slower oscillation state of 4 to 7 oscillation cycles per second. This is the state you experience in the twilight moments just as you are drifting off to sleep. It is also related to the subconscious state of mind. It is also connected with the deeper daydreaming states. In this state you will also have access to total dream recall, unlike in the Delta state.

4. **Delta** – the sleep state, where the brain waves oscillate at less than 4 cycles per second. It is the unconscious state of mind. Dreams are either

nonexistent in the delta state or usually not remembered.

When you tell someone to close their eyes and focus inwardly, you are leading them into the alpha state and perhaps even the theta state.

Alpha-Theta States and the Subconscious Mind

One of the best ways to connect with the subconscious mind is to find a way to enter the alpha and theta brain wave states. In the past thirty years several hypnosis practitioners have created hypnosis and meditation products to assist people in accessing these subconscious-related states.

Other ways to access these states include doing repetitive activities, as well as being in altered states related to times of increased physical sensation. Altered states include states of illness, as well as of heightened emotions, such as rage, fear, grief, hurt, happiness, and sexual arousal. These are prime times to access the subconscious mind. During these altered states, whatever you think and hear often bypasses the conscious mind and settles directly into the subconscious mind.

It is very difficult to maintain whatever transformed state has been created unless the subconscious mind is in agreement with and in acceptance of the new state. If the subconscious mind does not believe in the transformation, then it will find a way to go back to the original state. The human mind needs a certain amount of sameness and certainty.

The ego is also in charge of maintaining the status quo and is invested in keeping you alive. It is not, however, welcoming of change and new ideas.

8. The "Trance" and "Trans" in "Transformation"

According to Merriam-Webster online dictionary, the prefix "trans" of the word transformation means: "on or the other side of; across; beyond and through." [*www.merriam-webster.com/dictionary/trans*]. Thus, one of the meanings for transformation is one formation changing into another, such as wood becoming ash.

Trance means "a state of profound abstraction or absorption."

(*www.merriam-webster.com/dictionary/trance*).

When a person goes through a transformation, the person changes their sense of identity. The depth of the transformation correlates to the totality of the change in self-identity. If the transformation is not completely accepted by the subconscious mind, then the person will find himself or herself slipping back into the old identity. How often have you seen a person lose a large amount of weight only to gain it back within six months? This seems to be more likely if the transformation (in this case the weight loss) happens too quickly.

Unlike inanimate objects such as wood, which turn into ash through the process of burning, the human body can be affected by the psyche, which can cause the body return to its former state and maintain stasis.

This is why it is both necessary and important to apply techniques that connect you with your subconscious mind to support and maintain new transformations.

Support groups that acknowledge your new identity will help sustain it, as will meditation practices and audio recordings that guide you to connect with your subconscious mind.

In addition to the more familiar sitting meditations, there are also active meditations that assist people in going into trance to connect with their subconscious mind. For instance, there are several moving meditations associated with the controversial spiritual teacher and guru Osho, who is no longer in physical form. Osho thought that Americans and Westerners have minds that are often too agitated to be able to sit for long periods of time in stillness, so he and his musicians created a series of meditations, which you can find at *osho.com*.

Dance, movement and activities that impact the physical senses will activate the subconscious mind. In fact, scents directly impact the limbic system and activate memories.

Again, it is important to note that the most effective work for the person in trance involves focusing the person on the conscious questions and problems that thus far have not been resolved to your sense of satisfaction.

Another way that a people apply this principle of linking the conscious mind with the subconscious mind is by holding in their minds particular questions or issues to which they want answers just as they are drifting off to sleep. This is a helpful technique because their minds during sleep time is freer to access answers that may otherwise be inaccessible during a person's conscious state.

Bodywork and Twilight Time

Bodywork, such as Swedish Massage, Shiatsu and Thai Yoga Massage, can also bring up old memories that are stored in the subconscious. Jacob L. Moreno (1889 – 1974), the father of psychodrama states, "The body remembers what the mind forgets." [Dayton, Tian. Psychodrama *www.treatmentcenters.net/psychodrama.html*]

Bodywork sessions will often put the bodywork recipient in an altered state. This state can be likened to the state that Dave Czach, referred to in his article about Einstein.

Czach states: "It's been reported that Mr. Einstein said his best work resulted from ideas while engaging in 'something like' daydreaming . . . Wonderful solutions to almost any dilemma can be created while engaging in 'something like' daydreaming . . . When you daydream, physiological changes take place . . . What happened physiologically is your alpha brain waves became more dominant. According to twenty years of brain wave research by the late British biofeedback researcher C. Maxwell Cade, while in this 'light-alpha' state of mind, you become more relaxed. Ideas flow more easily . . . Mr. Einstein's 'something like' daydreaming level is known as the theta brain wave level. This state of mind is commonly referred to as the twilight zone."

("The Einstein Method to Rapid Solutions" Czach, Dave. 2003. *www.ofspirit.com/daveczach1.htm).*

9. Spells and the Subconscious

Before we go onto the homework for this week, let us look at voodoo spells and ways to dispel them. The reason we are exploring this topic is because spells usually lodge in the subconscious of the person who feels "under attack". This will be relevant when we explore ways to get off the Drama Triangle in *Chapter 5* – in particular, in regard to the Victim position, but here we look at the basic issue of clearing spells and overcoming victimhood.

A "spell" (according to the Merriam-Webster online dictionary is defined as:

  a: a spoken word or form of words held to have magic power.

  b: a state of enchantment; a strong compelling influence or attraction.

(*www.merriam-webster.com/dictionary/spell*).

Spells are literally created with words, intentions, and rituals. So, spells can literally be dispelled when you take apart the words of the spell, redirect the intentions, and do whatever sort of process reaches your own subconscious mind. You may have particular prayers that work for you. Or you may have particular dances, or other ways of creating a sort of initiation and demarcation process that is believed by your subconscious as well as your conscious mind.

Your conscious mind must also be involved in your transformation process. So, if you are so inclined, write out your intentions and keep track of the positive steps you take each day and night to accomplish your intentions.

To elaborate further ways to work with your conscious and subconscious minds, explore the following processes:

1. Stream of Consciousness Writing

2. Lucid Dreaming Exercises

3. Akashic Record Writing

4. Writing out a positive intention and then noticing what feelings emerge during your review of it. (If there are negative feelings, then it is important that you address these feelings to help your ego and psyche feel safe and willing to cooperate with your true self's positive intentions.)

10. Reverse Engineering

Although this term is usually associated with the analysis of equipment or computer programs (*en.wikipedia.org/wiki/Reverse_engineering*), it can ALSO be applied to personal transformation.

I was first introduced to the term in this context in one of Lisa Sassevich's three day training sessions (*www.lisasassevich.com*). In these sessions, she advised her participants to think about the results that they wanted to experience and then work backwards and find all the steps necessary to achieve their desired results.

Another way of conceptualizing this is to try to sell the excitement of the DESTINATION to your potential clients, as opposed to the processes used to achieve the destination. People usually become motivated to take action by becoming excited about what they will EXPERIENCE when they arrive at their desired destination.

So, think first about what you want to ACHIEVE and then find out what steps must be TAKEN to achieve the results you desire. It might be helpful to find people who are currently experiencing your desired outcome. Then find out what steps these role models took to achieve their successful results. This is also an example of what Tony Robbins calls "modeling" (*www.tonyrobbins.com*).

For example, I recently employed this principle to successfully complete a weight loss program. Anytime I would begin to feel discouraged with the slowness of the program, I would link into a Yahoo group connected with the specific weight loss program that I utilized. This Yahoo group contained before, during, and after photos of many other participants of this program. Thus by keeping my focus on the desired results and tapping into the successful results of many other people who followed the same steps as me, I was able to stick to the program and attain my own desired results. This is one of the approaches I use more generally to stay in the winning zone of life.

11. Homework to Create the Transformation You Desire

1. Write out a list of your top three desired outcomes.

2. For each outcome, write out a paragraph or two on how you would spend your entire day and evening when you have achieved your desired results. Include as many details as possible in this description.

3. To access the right side of your brain, you might also want to take a blank sheet of paper and draw a circle in the center that includes the statement of the desired outcome. Then create circles around the center circle and fill it with whatever thoughts come to mind about this desired outcome.

4. If there are negatives in the orbit of circles, then set up a plan that addresses each negative. Include both processes for your conscious mind and proactive steps and processes that will access your subconscious mind for achieving the desired outcome.

5. Look back and notice transformations you have made – skills you have learned, identities you have willing acquired, and define the steps that helped you make the specific transformations.

6. Keep a positive tracking journal and make daily notations of the things you did that day towards reaching your desired outcome. Even if you are only able to acknowledge small actions that are connected with this outcome, do so. Every step counts. As the Kahunas (Hawaiian shamans) say, "ENERGY FLOWS WHERE ATTENTION GOES!".

7. Search out mentors who model the behavior and circumstances that you desire to experience. Then take note of how they think and what they did to attain their status, as well as how they maintain it.

8. Most importantly, connect with an effective support system. This system may be an established support group connected with your community center, or it may be connected with a specific course.

9. If there is no system accessible to you (or even if there is), become a member of our B.E.S.T. System, and be open to the fulfillment of the things that you most desire to create in your life.

Part Two:

Additional Resources

Chapter Five: Drama Triangles and Relationships

Dr. Jacob L. Moreno created a series of techniques to help people heal on deep levels. One of most powerful techniques was the concept of the Drama Triangle. Here we are defining the Drama Triangle as a transactional model that contains three positions: victim, persecutor and rescuer. One of Moreno's most memorable quotes is:

"The body remembers what the mind forgets."

(Moreno quote – Dayton article, www.asgpp.org/html/article1.html)

Dr. Moreno, a Romanian born psychiatrist who lived from 1889 to 1974 (*en.wikipedia.org/wiki/Jacob_L._Moreno*), is considered the father of psychodrama (*en.wikipedia.org/wiki/Psychodrama*). His work has helped many people access and heal emotional material that otherwise would have remained inaccessible. Since his initial work, there have been a number of therapists such as Gay and Katie Hendricks, as well as Dr. Tian Dayton who have taken Dr. Moreno's work into greater public realms of recognition. Dr. Dayton's work helped me to explore the aspects of the Drama Triangle in a deeper way.

While I was in a coaching certification program with Gay and Katie Hendricks, I first experienced the power of the Drama Triangle. While I was exploring the basic structure of it, many questions emerged for me, such as: "How do I get off of it and stay off of it?" These questions led me to explore the internal scripts that are present for people while they are on each position of the Triangle.

The Triangle also helps connect people with gestures and non-verbal right-brained experiences, which are associated with the various positions of the Triangle. As Dayton puts it, "Gesturing is our first language. It is the mind-body communication upon which all subsequent language is built. Before language formally enters the picture, we have learned a rich tapestry of gestures to communicate our needs and desires. This gesturing comprises a nonverbal communication that informs our ability to express ourselves and understand others throughout our lives." (Dayton, *The Living Stage*, p. xvii).

The next pages contain segments from the transcript of the course session where my students were intrigued as well as helped by our explorations of this universal triangle.

1. The Three Positions

Drama Triangle

Persecutor **Martyr**

Victim

We will now explore the positions of the Drama Triangle:

1. Victim
2. Persecutor
3. Martyr.

There is a Drama Triangle game that we will play that will help us understand the negative and positive self-talk related to each position. We will also explore ways to get off and stay off the potential drama triangles in our lives.

Faces of Victim – I referred to this last week when I mentioned Robert Dilt's work with helping his mother transform her limiting beliefs, so she was able to live fifteen years longer after she had received a "death sentence" from her doctor. He also wrote some articles on how Jesus healed and worked with beliefs, and how part of what He was doing involved the fact that when somebody came to Him, they were usually feeling hopeless, helpless, or worthless.

So that does also involve the Drama Triangle. We are going to work with some information involving that. Stephen Karpman was actually the one who termed it the "Drama Triangle".

(*www.karpmandramatriangle.com* 2010)

Lyn Forest has also written some great information on it (*www.lynneforrest.com/html/the_faces_of_victim.html* 2008).

You can see that there are different entry points (gateways) to it. So you might enter it as a **Victim**, **Persecutor** (aka Villain), or **Rescuer** (aka Martyr). The Victim is the lowest position on the Triangle. The other two positions are one up from the Victim (and feel superior to him/her).

The Rescuer Is The Caretaker – they are usually disregarding what is important to them personally and are instead just looking outward and becoming a Martyr as they do it. This leads them to become a Victim. We enter on one position, but we rotate through all of the positions as we are on the Triangle.

Let's examine characteristics of people on the starting gate of the Persecutor – They identify primarily with the Victim, and they feel they are justified, as in the "tit for tat" that Lisa was talking about. Your friend feels justified in giving the person the same type of behavior because she feels she was harmed in some way. And the best way to get back at the other person is "tit for tat".

Victims believe that they can't take care of themselves and that they are unable to handle life.

These roles were created during the years we spent in our family of origin, where we had caretakers who usually interacted with us in such a way that we were all on the Drama Triangle. And then we take that Drama Triangle to current situations as well as to memories of past situations.

So, the roles become unconscious core beliefs, which were derived from our interpretations of early family encounters, and then they become life themes. Have you heard somebody tell you over and over again how he or she is a victim? Has anybody had that experience?

Edna: I have heard people say, "It always happens to me."

Terry: Right, that is very much Victim language. "It happens to me," versus "I am involved in this." It happens to me – that is a way of knowing that one is in a role of Victim. Or if someone is in Persecutor role, they will be, "I'm justified in doing this because I had a certain experience" . . . and so I am justified in retaliating.

The Blister Story

So before we actually address that, I brought these handy little forms with Victim, Martyr, and Villain on them. And I am going to show you how this works, and then I want you to experience this for yourself. So this is where the Blister Story comes in . . .

I had a great weekend and I was wondering how I could really demonstrate the process of the positions on the triangle. So I thought, OK, I can tell you my own victim story:

As I said, I had a great weekend, and I was really busy. I was employed on Saturday night for the Northwestern Thai Fever Festival where I was one of the Shiatsu/Thai Yoga therapists. And it was really fun. It was nonstop event and I worked the concession with one other person. We were paid for it and had a good time.

There were lots of food and festivities. I met lots of people. There were people who came with their families and one or more members would receive a session. Tina and I were offering mini-sessions. And Shiatsu is a type of bodywork that works with meridians and acupressure points, and Thai Yoga works with deep stretches, in essence helping a person relax and release tension.

I had a great time working the event. And then the next morning I was scheduled to sing here at Unity. I had to be here for the eight o'clock rehearsal, and then we were giving two performances, for the 9:30 and 11:30 services. However, late Saturday evening I received a disturbing email from somebody who was really unsettled and, as a result, I didn't sleep that well that night. Also, I had to work the Green Fest on Sunday afternoon. At the time I had agreed to do the Green Festival I thought that I would be driving downtown with another person, which would have made logistics more manageable.

Sunday was a really hot day. I had told the organizer of the booth for Green Fest that I was willing to do it on the condition that the other person would be driving. However, it turned out that this other person would NOT be driving after all. The organizer, however, said to me, "You really have to work it. We don't have anyone else." So I said, "OK, OK, I'll do it."

So I really overextended myself, AND it was really hot, and I was really depleted. When I got there the parking was awful downtown and I was thinking, "I don't want to pay the big bucks." So, I was hurrying there and I was just going, "I'm overtired, I'm overstimulated. But I'm doing this because I can't get out of it."

So it was like being a Martyr because I was upset that I was getting blisters on my feet. And then I was being the Villain because I got there late and other people had to stay longer to cover for me. When I got there, one person was able to leave and the other person was able to take a break and get some bodywork, but I didn't stay the whole time and I was going, "Well, they should have heard me. They didn't hear me say that I didn't want to do this without the other person giving me a ride."

I was in the Villain role because I wasn't able to be fully present for them. So the whole time I was going to different positions on the Triangle. And I have the blisters on my feet from hurrying to the Green Fest to show you that I was definitely on this triangle because I wasn't in the center of taking care of myself, or observing this triangle, or setting boundaries. But we will talk about that – how to get off of it. But, in the meantime, I want you to come up here. Who would like to do the Triangle?

Bret: With what?

Terry: Anything. You can do it based on feeling jealous if you want. What would your starting point be? My starting point was Victim. I was feeling definitely overwhelmed and put upon.

Bret: My starting point is going to be the Martyr.

Terry: So, what is your internal dialogue? Take a situation.

Bret: I have to always be present for my sister, no matter how outrageous her behavior is.

Terry: OK, so while you are doing that, how do you become Villain?

Bret: I become the Villain by cutting short conversations, not being available, not giving her what she wants.

Terry: So you are withholding. And then, Victim – how do you become Victim?

Bret: Then I become so remorseful and depressed that I lose all objectivity. I can't stand aside and look objectively at this encounter between the two of us. And so then I have lots of angst.

Terry: Thank you, that was great.

Myra: Where should I start? This is about my daughter and me. Let's see, Martyr. I am doing all those things for her, cooking, giving her money and she is so . . . We went to Starved Rock this weekend. It's hot and she is playing loud music. And she wants to stop off and I am like playing the Victim. I'm not saying anything; I am keeping my mouth shut. I want us to have a good relationship. And then I become like the Villain; I tell her – you know I want to tell her, "You know you broke my heart so many

	times. You know you don't even care about how I feel"... and then I ruined it.
Terry:	Thank you; that was a perfect example of the Drama Triangle.
Edna:	I am babysitting two of my grandchildren. My daughter won't tell me how long she is going to be away. I can barely stay awake. Their daddy comes home and he says, "I'm tired and I'm going to take a rest," and he goes and he lies down and I am feeling worse and worse like I am going to maybe faint. So I say, "Rudy, wake up, get out of bed, I'm leaving."
Lila:	Yesterday morning I agreed to go on an appointment with my husband; however, it meant that I would have to drive him to work, and then I would have to use my time to work on my business somewhere in the area where his work place is until we could then go on to another appointment together. So, I did that. He gets into the car and he had made a business call and he said something to that person that could have been said just a little bit differently. And I said to him, perhaps you could have said it this other way. And then he said, I don't care what you say. So I thought that I was being instructive and he thought I was being the Villain. Then at that point, I thought, I'm done for the day.

2. Getting Off the Drama Triangle

Terry:	Perfect example. Our lives are about the stories we create about our past and our future. And as we change our stories, our life changes too.
	So there are some ways you can get off of it. First you have to notice you are on it. Come back to your

own center, and breathe through the feelings that are coming up, the feelings of anger of giving your time away when you didn't want to give your time away. Get in touch with the feeling of being hurt when some mean things were said to you. It will help you clear the emotional pain by breathing through the feelings to let them pass through you. All of these feelings are giving you signals of how your life is. Welcome all of these feelings because all feelings give you valuable bio-survival related information. And it is really a matter of how you take in the feelings, how you take in the information and how you are proactive with it. So that is also exploring your responses.

Edna: Didn't we all start at Martyr?

Terry: I didn't. I'm overwhelmed. I don't want to do this. I wasn't heard. So those are my limiting beliefs that came up. So, we have gone through the recapitulation.

So, you can give this story a new resolution, i.e., a new Act Three. And that will be really important. But you were saying, Marvin, "I love myself too much to do X, Y, or Z, to be with somebody where I might then get sick." OK, be compassionate with yourself, and then give new meaning to the story. Let that story inform you of different ways to be.

I thought about the Blister Story and thought, "You know, it's really my responsibility to either find somebody else to ride to Navy Pier with or to say to them, 'Look, I'll do it, and I need you to help out with the parking. I am not going to walk twenty-five minutes and get blisters,'" not that I knew then that I was going to get blisters. I needed to say, "Nope; that was not my agreement." There were lots of options that I could have had, that I didn't take. As it was, things turned out fine. There was somebody who stayed there. I did some work while I was there and it was OK. It wasn't my ideal situation but it was a learning experience.

Recognize when you are on a Drama Triangle, and choose healthy boundaries and nutrition. There are people now saying that you need to nourish your brain so that your brain thinks clearly. In my situation the heat was really hard on me, so I needed to look at that because I was feeling extra depletion. I needed to look at what could I do so I would feel better about the situation.

Robert Dilts talks about the way Jesus healed. Healing has to do with the words "I-am-I", which have to do with curing or repairing and healing and being therapeutic. He was able to address people's limiting beliefs. And He was able to engage them in such a way that He was able to bypass their conscious minds, and really help them come into a place of healing. He was able to help them begin to feel hopeful when they felt hopeless. Where they felt helpless, he found a way to help them feel capable and responsible and where they felt worthless, he helped them feel worthy and have a sense of belonging.

"If thou canst believe, all things are possible to him that believeth." *Mark 9:24*

Recognize the beliefs and how he opened up people's psyches to realize that more is possible than what they had understood to be true.

"According to your faith be it unto you." *Matthew 9:29*

Your experiences are a reflection of your internal beliefs. We went through how we delete, generalize, and distort. So what we are focusing on is what will determine how we think about and talk about our experiences. Does that make sense?

He was a master at helping people work with beliefs and helping them work through their limitations to help them gain a sense of healing and completeness.

We are talking about the positions of the Triangle. This is a part of life. It is a part of all stories that have beginnings, middles, and ends. If you have ever studied screenplays, the first act is going along and all of a sudden they have a challenge and Act Two begins when the person says, "OK, I am going to work with this challenge. I am going to overcome whatever is going on." And then Act Three is the resolution in classic movies.

There are some movies that don't have resolutions. But we are talking about classic stories that have empowered and sustained humankind and inspired us. When we can stand in the middle, when we can get off the positions, we can be more objective and create resolutions and happier endings to our own stories – but first we have to notice we are on it [the Triangle]. As long as we are on it, chances are we will be going through all of the positions.

First, notice you are on it, take a breath, and feel the feelings, because these are core feelings. For me it didn't just start with that time that I wasn't feeling heard or respected or feeling overextended. It started at a much younger time in my life. Does that make sense? So, I need to feel the core structure if I am going to keep staying off of the Drama Triangle.

Externally too, I can look at it and get some perspective and distance. Like right now, I am looking at it and telling you about it. I'm looking at it saying, "That was a story and I'm not sticking to it. I am giving it a more empowered meaning and I am using it to teach an important concept."

Actually, I learned this concept in a seminar facilitated by Gay and Katie Hendricks when I was getting my certification in the Mind-Body Vibrancy Course.

Emotional Mastery – we will go over this later. It's basically, understanding emotions, having ease, being able to go between emotions, and being able to express them in a clear way. When we are on these positions we go into the generalizations, distortions, and deletions. So it's really important to be able to express them. I need to be able to go, "I realize I was having a hard time with this and I feel as though you didn't hear me." These are the different ways that you can work with the modalities that are connected with your internal representations of the world.

It is important to understand that emotions mean certain things. For instance, jealously has to do with feeling that there is a loss, and something is being threatened.

There are times to know when it is appropriate to be patient and determined. It is important to be able to sort out who we are, versus what our behavior is and what we are feeling. Sometimes we feel badly about ourselves because we clump together who we are, what we are feeling, and what we are doing.

Sort these out. Then we can start addressing each one. You know if I am feeling depressed, it doesn't mean that my core is any less, it may just mean that I may need to do things to address the depletion.

Breathe through the states, understanding them and making proactive decisions.

Notice that your language is connected with Victim, Villain and Martyr.

What goal would you like to experience this week? Choose a goal buddy and say what you would like to experience this week and how you will know you have experienced it. Keep it concise.

Myra: I am going to accomplish a financial goal this week.

Edna: I would like to plant flowers and clean my deck.

Bret: I want to be more proactive for myself; if something comes up that is negative or painful in any relationship, on any level, I will recognize that it is happening. And just say, "Ouch."

Terry: And take a deep breath, so you can breathe through it.

Lila: To remind myself that I can always choose to tap into the empowered part of myself.

Marvin: I have a meeting coming up a week from Sunday and I want to do the agenda for it.

Terry: And for me: to write fifteen pages. And one last thing . . . name one thing that you experienced tonight that will make a difference for you this week.

Edna: That I can change; I can go from "I can't" to "I can".

Terry: Yes, you can. Thank you.

Myra: More focused.

Bret: Just this Victim/Villain/Martyr triangle is really interesting. And it is going to be fun for me at any given time to see where I am.

Terry: Thank you.

Lila: It's just a reminder that with my new career, my husband's new career, that it's OK for us not to be as codependent as we were in our former profession, and I can enjoy it.

Terry: You might even say that it is OK to be more independent.

And I have a homework assignment for all of you this week, that you notice your Drama Triangles. You are welcome to notice other people's triangles, but you really can't do anything about them other than say to yourself, "You are on it." But you can do that for yourself, too. When you are on it, breathe through your feelings. You might even want to note down when you are on it. And come back next week and share a story with us . . .

Thank you. This was great. We didn't get to the movies, but we didn't need them. We were our own little movies tonight. So thank you, thank you, and I will see you here next week.

After this session, my students requested more material on the Drama Triangle, so at the next session I presented the following segments of material, much of which is based on the work of Lynne Forrest. (*www.lynneforrest.com/html/the_faces_of_victim.html*):

Terry: Each position [of the Triangle] is accompanied by dysfunctional internal dialogue. These are unconscious core beliefs acquired in childhood, derived from our interpretation of early family encounters. These become "life themes" that predispose us towards the unconscious selection of a particular starting gate position on the Triangle. Our starting gate position on the Victim triangle is not only where we most often enter the triangle, it is also the role through which we actually define ourselves.

As mentioned, the Rescuer and the Persecutor start in a position that's one up from the Victim position.

The Starting Gate Rescuers/Martyrs (SGR's) see themselves as "helpers" and "caretakers". They need someone to rescue (Victim) in order to feel vital and important. It's difficult for SGR's to recognize themselves as ever having been in a Victim position – they're the ones with the answers after all. They need to feel vital, needed and able to fix the situation. It is difficult for them to identify and acknowledge their own needs. They will end up rotating to both of the other positions.

Starting Gate Persecutors/Villains (SGP's), on the other hand, identify themselves primarily as Victims. They are usually in complete denial about their blaming tactics. When it is pointed out to them, they argue that an attack is warranted and necessary for self-protection.

These two – the Rescuer and the Persecutor – are the two opposite extremes of the Victim. They assume a "one-up" position over others, i.e., they relate as though they are better, stronger, smarter, or more together than the victim.

Starting Gate Victims (SGV's) believe they cannot take care of themselves. They see themselves as consistently unable to handle life.

More on the Rescuer position:

They need someone to rescue in order to feel vital and important. They have difficulty recognizing themselves in the Victim position because they have all the answers.

This is the shadow aspect of the mother principle. Because of giving appropriate expression of support and nurturing, the Rescuer tends to smother, control and manipulate others "for their own good."

This is a classic co-dependent person who wants to "fix it."

Rescuing is an addiction that comes from an unconscious need to feel valued.

SGR's usually grow up in families where their dependency needs are not acknowledged . . . Their needs are negated and so they tend to treat themselves with the same degree of negligence that they experienced as children.

"If I take care of them long enough, then, sooner or later, they will take care of me, too." The resulting disappointment sends the SGR spiraling into depression.

Betrayed, used, and hopeless are trademark feelings of the Victim phase of a Starting Gate Rescuer's dance around the triangle. An SGR's greatest fear is that they will end up alone.

Authentic helpers act without expectations for reciprocation. They empower rather than disable those they serve and encourage self-reliance and taking responsibility for getting one's own needs met.

CREATE A NEW SCRIPT FOR THIS POSITION NOW!

If a person is on the position of Rescuer, what can he say to himself that will help him take care of himself in a healthy way rather than just blame the Victim for not giving him what he wants?

Kathy: I can rescue myself?

Terry: Yes, you can rescue yourself. And rather than the Rescuer feeling like they are just rescuing that person, maybe they can help that person become capable and empowered because Rescuers are often afraid of being alone. That is one of their biggest fears.

What can the rescuer do that to help them take care of themselves?

Kathy: I can rescue myself.

Terry: Yes, and maybe they can help the person become capable and empowered.

Kathy: Is it like a contract?

Terry: It's an expectation, but it usually doesn't work that well.

Persecutors have also had shame-based experiences in their childhood. They tend to have been in situations where they were abused. They were neglected. They were made to feel worthless. So they overcome this by overpowering others. And that helps them not look at their own vulnerability. So their fear is that they will be vulnerable. So they fight hard not to be vulnerable. And they need to be able to accept that they are not powerful 100% of the time, or invulnerable 100% of the time.

Self-accountability is really the only way to get off the Triangle.

Starting Gate Persecutors identify themselves primarily as Victims, and they are in denial about their blaming tactics. When it is pointed out to them, they assert that it was necessary.

Like the Rescuer, this role is also shame-based and is most often taken on by someone who received overt mental and/or physical abuse during their childhood. They are often secretly seething inside from a shame-based wrath that ends up running their lives. For survival sake, they repress deep-seated feelings of worthlessness. They hide their pain behind a facade of indignant wrath and uncaring detachment.

The Persecutor position is the "shadow father" principle. A healthy father's job is to protect and provide for his family. The SGP attempts to "reform" and discipline those around him by using manipulation and brute force.

SGP's overcome feelings of helplessness and shame by overpowering others. Their methods include bullying, preaching, threatening, blaming, lecturing, interrogating, and outright attack. They believe in getting even, very often through aggressive acts. The Persecutor needs someone to blame. They are in denial that their methods are hurtful. Self-honesty feels like self-blame. They deny their vulnerability. Their fear is that they are powerless.

SELF-ACCOUNTABLITY IS THE ONLY WAY OFF THE TRIANGLE!

So what could be a way to create an empowering statement for somebody who is in the persecutor position?

CREATE AN EMPOWERING SCRIPT FOR THIS POSITION NOW!

Kathy: I am accountable. I am accountable to others and myself?

Terry: Yes.

Kathy: Is what's behind that sort of like "I can't beat up on everybody"?

Terry: Well, if they are not willing to feel their own vulnerability, they will tend to blame others and judge others and often act out the abuse they felt and feel justified in seeking revenge and justice. They need someone to blame. They are in a cycle of needing to get even. Jill, you are shaking your head. Does this make sense to you?

Jill: It's hilarious – it is absolutely, precisely the dynamics of my previous relationship.

Terry: See? Your unconscious told you that you had to be here. Good call.

First of all, as mentioned, the Persecutor is the shadow element of the father principle. Does that make sense? So rather than being a father who is really guiding and disciplining in a healthy way, he is condemning and judging.

Also, as mentioned, the position of Rescuer is the shadow element of the mother principle. They are manipulating and controlling to make themselves indispensible to somebody. So, that is not a healthy way that is a shadow principle. Does that make sense?

Consider the Victim. What has happened is that this type of person has survived by being helpless and not feeling capable, and feeling like they are intrinsically damaged. They will often sabotage the Rescuer's efforts. If somebody tries to guide them they will go, "Yes, but . . . ".

Here are some quotes from Lynne Forrest about the Victim position, and its relationship to the other positions:

"This is the shadow aspect of wounded child – the part that is vulnerable, needy and innocent. And the child self does need support on occasion but when this person becomes convinced that he/she can't take care of him/herself, this person moves into Victim position. They often believe that they are intrinsically damaged and incapable."

"So, they deny their problem-solving abilities and their potential for self-generated power. They often see themselves as broken and unfixable."

"The very thing a Rescuer seeks (**validation** and **appreciation**) is the thing Victims most resent giving, because it is a reminder to them of their own deficiencies."

> "For a Victim to move to Persecutor on the Triangle usually means sabotaging the efforts made to rescue them, often through passive-aggressive behavior. For example, they are skilled at playing a game called, 'Yes, but . . .'."
>
> "They live in a perpetual shame spiral, often leading to self-abuse of drugs, alcohol and food, gambling, etc."
>
> "They are often identified as the problem of their family."
>
> "Victims must learn to assume responsibility for themselves and initiate self-care."
>
> "They must challenge the ingrained belief that they can't take care of themselves."

Kathy: Can you be on more than one position?

Terry: If you are on this triangle, you will go through all the positions, but you will tend to have a starting gate, a place where you tend to start. You will tend to have a theme for all of these triangles.

So, what could the victim say that would give them an empowered script internally and externally?

Marvin: "I can take care of myself."

Terry: Yes, "I can take care of myself," and maybe, "I am learning to take care of myself," because all of these are like learning to walk. You can get them like this [snap of the fingers], and you can also go through the steps. If you have ever watched toddlers learning to walk, you see that if they fall they don't go, "You should have done that better." What do they do? They get up and they try it again. But as adults we tend to judge and criticize. We take on a critical voice. But it is that getting up and doing it again, and watching and letting the mirror neurons help out that will help a person learn to walk.

So, how do we get off this cycle? The Rescuer, Persecutor, and Victim. They all end up as Victim because people aren't really feeling their feelings in a healthful way.

But there are two empowered places. Say them:

1. Centered

2. Observer.

The truth is you really want to be able to be in the center position, which means you have to be willing to feel your feelings and become accountable for them. So rather than saying, "You made me angry," you can say, "This event triggered my anger and I can be proactive with it." Or, "This event triggered hurt in me and I really need to feel it and then make a healthy choice."

Thereby we can replace what we tend to do with distortions, deletions, and generalizations like, "You always make me angry," and "You always step on my foot." It is important to take off the filters.

It is important to be able to be in the observation position – so you can observe it and learn from it. Give these triangle experiences new meanings for yourself.

Developing Emotional Mastery Skills

- Understanding of emotions
- Ease and flexibility in expression

- Knowing when and when not to express emotions
- Knowing how to express them
- Understanding their messages
- Being proactive with their messages
- Breathing into the emotions so they can flow through you.

These emotions are very innate core survival mechanisms that we have that are really meant to help us survive in life and help us get through the challenging times.

Emotional mastery means having flexibility and ease and appropriate expression of your emotions.

Ways to Work with Emotions:

1. Breathing into them.
2. Embracing them and letting them pass through your being.
3. Transformative decisions.
4. Proactive behaviors.
5. Choosing new emotional states.

You may also like to read a very helpful book on emotions titled *The Emotional Hostage: Rescuing Your Emotional Life*, by Leslie Cameron-Bandler.

The unconscious mind is always active in all of the Drama Triangle positions. Being aware of this will give you pathways into understanding these positions, as will being aware of your phrases, gestures, and feelings.

Set a goal for what you want to experience this week and check in with a "buddy" about your goal and what you will do to achieve it. I recommend that you make a goal of taking each position and write out an empowered sentence for each position, just like we did tonight.

How will you know you have done this? You will have written down your empowered sentences beforehand. Sometimes when you are in one of these drama triangle positions, you find that it is difficult to be resourceful on the spot. You might find yourself struggling to find the right words. You can't speak, set your own boundaries or say what is really going on. There may not be much validation and encouragement for you to speak up.

If for instance, when you feel anger, somebody might say to you, "You shouldn't feel that way," However, if you have written out your sentences in advance, you might find it a bit easier to feel resourceful on the spot. When you do accept your feelings with compassion, rather than judgment, it will be much easier to breathe into the feelings and let them pass through you so that you may then choose the next more resourceful thoughts and feelings.

Terry: So, I want you to turn to a buddy right now and talk about how you will work with what you have learned tonight, how you would write out new, empowering scripts for your Drama Triangle positions.

I would like to have each of you describe something that was significant for you this evening.

Kathy: The Drama Triangle positions were really powerful, because I saw myself in shame and regret and I am trying to transform that, but I saw the dynamics of it.

Terry: Come back and we will work on the empowered sentences and scripts for these positions. It is really important to create actual sentences and scripts

	that help you move your life forward. Thanks for sharing this, and thank you for being here. Jill, what did you get?
Jill:	Pretty much the same thing. It was like shockingly clear.
Terry:	Shockingly clear! So what are you going to do with it this week?
Jill:	I think, be in the observational position to see where I pick up and see the dynamics and go, "Oh!," and then to me there was almost like this bizarre humor. If you step back, you can go, "And that's what that is? That's silly". But it feels so serious and significant and heavy when you don't understand it. But once you have a construct for it, it's like, "Oh."
Bret:	Yeah.
Terry:	Right. So we are going to give you more constructs of how to speak when you are on a position and how to speak to the people in the other positions who are on the Triangle with you. Does that make sense? That is really important.
Marvin:	I said earlier. That we really attach meaning to people and that we can control that. So, if we think we are helpless, we just go with the flow of everything that comes into our lives. So, I guess I am going to be very careful of the meanings I attach to my situations.
Terry:	Wonderful! So, you are going to be empowered with the meanings you attach.
Jill:	If I can take what Myra said and what Kathy said and blend it together, it is actually really very cool. It was the exercise wearing masks, because what is

happening in the Triangle, nothing is actually in this present moment, it is really the trigger. You looking like someone else, maybe like my mother, is what is triggering the structure of the Triangle. It's not you really, which is huge.

Terry: Yes, it has been buried. It has been subconscious until this point.

Jill: If Kathy reminds me of someone negative, I would have a hard time feeling good about Kathy until I worked on that.

Terry: Until you got present with Kathy and took the filters off of the deletion, distortion, and generalization.

Jill: To get out of the triangle that I might have started with Kathy even though it doesn't have anything to do with Kathy.

Edna: I am intrigued by the concept of being centered. If I am centered and know where I am in the Triangle, I may be observing and that would resolve my position.

Terry: Play with this idea this week and see how that works for you. It is entirely possible that it will work really well for you. Thank you. And work on the scripts for each position. Observe the position and come up with a script for each position.

Jill: Is there a different language for each position depending on the entry point?

Terry: Yes. Because the language needs are different. The Persecutor wants to justify and punish. The Rescuer wants to take care of and have a dependency. The Victim wants to be taken care of.

Bret: Well what is really interesting is that last week you had each of us stand on each position. And what is interesting is that you can be in relationship with someone and you can go from one spot to another in just an instant.

Terry: Right.

Bret: They are almost like the flip side of the coin, a three-sided coin.

Terry: Right. I am proud of all of you for getting out of the shame-based Triangles by the statements you constructed tonight, by learning this process, by letting your unconscious be present.

Bret: What's interesting is that when you look at it analytically, and you are saying what you said a couple of minutes ago. You don't feel the shame because you are analyzing it, whereas when you are living it, there is shame.

Terry: Who is feeling it?

Bret: I am feeling the shame.

Terry: Very good. You got that tonight.

I am proud of all of you for getting out of the shame-based Triangles by the statements you constructed tonight, by learning this process, by letting your unconscious and conscious be present, and by participating fully and being really open minded to all of this and willing to work with each other, too.

Thank you. Have a blessed empowered wonderful week.

Kathy: Is there a quick answer, if someone else is locked onto a position. Is there a way to take care of it?

Terry: Notice what position you are on and take care of yourself, because if you are doing that, they can't stay on that position and if they do stay on one of the positions, it is still for them to work through. But each of these positions is designed to teach you how to take care of yourself by understanding the needs that are innately embedded in each position. So, thank you for tonight.

Tian Dayton, whom we have discussed previously in regard to emotional literacy in *Chapter Three*, also addresses psychological health by recommending another way to deal with conflicts that arise in relationships and Drama Triangles. She points out that psychological health doesn't mean that two people will never get into conflict. Rather, "Health means that they will be able to step back, regroup and go through the steps of emotional literacy to find their way out of it." (Dayton, *Trauma and Addiction*, p.172)

She suggests that people are able to facilitate healing by:

1. **Naming the emotion:** Develop skills to define and name each emotion that is present during the conflict.

2. **Decoding the meaning you gave it as a child:** Notice what meanings you attached to these emotions that are reflective of the emotions you experienced during childhood conflicts. Explore the contexts and childhood meanings.

3. **Being proactive choice of healthful reaction:** Realize that you are no longer a child and can now make healthier choices. Rather than act on the knee jerk reactions associated with the triggered

emotions, breathe into the feelings, pause by counting to ten, and allow yourself to create a more empowering context and meaning for the emotions you are currently experiencing.

Transformation is not complete unless the transformation also evolves, maintaining the shift from the negative emotional associations from the former state to maintaining the positive emotions of the newly evolved state. In order to maintain and expand your transformation it is important to set up a consistent and healthy support system that helps you continue to feel into your emotions to receive their vital messages, and then make more empowering choices on a daily basis.

Chapter Six: Recapitulation for Transformation

1. Recapitulation

Recapitulation is a spiritual technique that helps you call back whatever energy you unintentionally (or intentionally) dispersed or gave away. You may have experienced the power of recapitulation to call back your dispersed energy and seal up any potential energy leaks. As well as helping to retrieve your energy, it also helps you to release any and all unwanted energy that may have been projected or imprinted onto your energy system. This process allows you to unhook from past traumatic relationships, situations, and events.

I first discovered this technique when I read Tasha Abelar's book *The Sorcerer's Crossing: a Woman's Journey*. Since that time, I further researched the techniques through Internet searches, and then developed a variation of my own that has been very helpful for my own life and the lives of my clients and students.

Here are the steps:

1. Close your eyes and visualize the event and/or situation about which you still feel a charge of energy and a lack of satisfactory resolution.

2. Then, as if you are sucking through a straw call back your energy from that event, person, place, and/or

thing by inhaling and visualizing/imagining that all of the energy that you had dispersed at the original time of the trauma is now being returned to you from all seen and unseen dimensions.

3. Once you have called back this energy, complete the inhalation by swallowing and imaging that this newfound recalled energy is now settling within your core being. Affirm that it is being recollected through an energy filter system that brings in only the energy that is authentically your own energy, free and clear of any and all distortions from other people, places, and beings.

4. Then take your right hand (if you are right-handed; otherwise, your left) and with your index finger and middle finger cut away all cords that are connected to that person and situation. Remember that you are utilizing your imagination (and perhaps visualization) skills to accomplish this cord-cutting process. It is important to affirm that the love remains, but all distortions and negative energy connected to that situation are cleared away from your energy field.

5. Then state out loud, "That was then, this is now. I now allow myself to be complete now and from this moment on."

6. After this process, it is often helpful to imagine that there is a sphere of light surrounding your entire energy field. This sphere of light is constructed in such a way that there are energy mirrors covering the entire outside surface of the sphere. These mirrors allow all energy that is not congruent with your authentic self to bounce off of your sphere, rather than penetrate into your inner field. I liken this process to standing inside your home and

looking out the window and seeing rain on the outside rather than the inside of your space. You can see it and hear it but it does not penetrate into your home. Instead, you remain dry, comfortable, and protected. .

7. It is also helpful to imagine that there is a sphere of light surrounding the entire energy field around the people and the situations from which you have called back your energy. This sphere of light is constructed similarly to the sphere that you have placed around yourself; HOWEVER, instead of the mirrors facing outward, construct the mirrors covering the entire *inside* surface of the sphere. Thus, whatever negative energy this person or situation tries to project outward, will only bounce back to them.

8. It is important to remember that traumatic experiences often nestle into our beings in layers. Even if you have performed one recapitulation on a specific memory and situation, it may take more than one time to clear away all of the past charged, entangled energy that was projected and imprinted into your field of thoughts, feelings, memories, and experiences.

You may also want to practice this technique with another person and/or a group of people who hold the focus of this process with you – because when two or more people focus on the same thing, the energy is intensified.

2. Reclaiming Lost Parts of Your Soul

It is important to reclaim the energy we have intentionally or inadvertently attached to a loved one who has died. Reclaiming the parts we gave to past love relationships, as well as reclaiming the energy from people, places, and things will help you feel more complete and retain more of your vital energy.

Saying goodbye to a loved one who has transitioned out of their body can often be traumatic and draining. It seems to be human nature to unconsciously send part of our own energy to the loved one who is departing this earth plane. There is a misconception that sending our energy with the one who has left their body may make their afterlife journey easier. This is particularly true for parents who must say goodbye to a child that has died.

Utilizing this process to help you retrieve your own energy will be the most beneficial way to live for yourself and the departed loved one. Surely the one you loved wants to know that you are surviving and thriving. Hence, if you feel that your thoughts are still bound up with the spirit of one who has departed your life, you should work with the recapitulation process to reclaim your energy. This will help ease any depression that may have followed the departure of your loved one.

This concept also applies to past romantic relationships where you experienced giving a lot of your energy to your partner as well as taking on their energy. In the long run, your past partner and you will both feel better when you have reclaimed your own energy and returned their energy to them.

If you are in the process of clearing the clutter out of your home and life, it is also helpful to work with the process of recapitulation, because in many cases the objects that are in your home and life contain memories associated with your acquiring and utilizing these objects. Remember everything is made up of energy; therefore, it is much easier to let go of an object once you have reclaimed the energy you had given that object to maintain its presence in your life.

Reclaiming the energy you have given to places in order to stay connected to them can also be an empowering process. Remember you can still keep the gratitude and love for these people, places, and things. The only thing you are releasing is the energy charge and entanglement that had been connected all of them.

Chapter Seven: Trinities of Manifestation

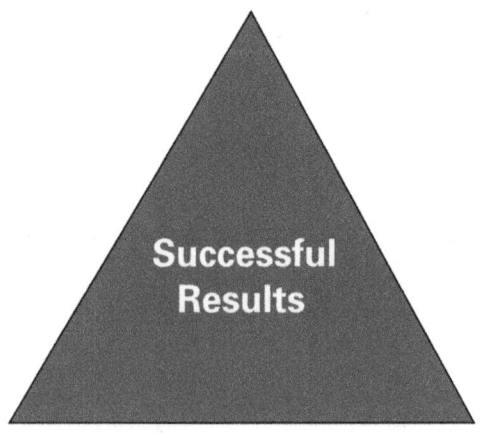

1. Thoughts, Feelings and Actions

By now you have seen how the these three elements of thought, feelings and actions are meant to be in alignment in order for you to experience true manifestation on all levels of reality. The intention of this book is to assist you in accessing and empowering these three dynamics of the manifestation triangle.

2. Ethereal, External and Internal Teams

The next chart is a variation on this "Manifestation Trinity". By connecting with these three aspects of manifestation and bringing them into congruency and harmony with each other, you will be able to accelerate your rate of successful manifestations.

In this chart:

Ethereal Team: Spiritual Practices – Meditation, Prayer...

External Team: Prayer Groups, Mastermind Groups...

Internal Team: Your Belief Systems in Your Conscious and Subconscious Minds.

Trinity of Manifestation

Ethereal Team

External Team   Internal Team

Chapter Eight: Putting It All Together

Now that you have reached this point in this course, it's time to put it all together and implement strategies to keep your transformations alive AND continue your progress.

1. Stress Management

We have set the foundation for this work by creating a clear idea of what you want to create in your life as well as establishing ongoing powerful stress management practices. To review, these techniques involve:

1. Breath management techniques.

2. Switching your internal thoughts from negative self-talk thoughts to positive self-talk thoughts.

3. Short-term goal setting.

4. Mental rehearsal.

2. Emotional Literacy

Once you have established these powerful practices, it is important to stay committed to evolving your emotional literacy skills (see the *Emotional Literacy* section in *Chapter Three*):

1. Breathing into your emotions as they arise in the moment.

2. Receiving the information embedded in these emotions.

3. Assigning more empowering meanings to these emotions. Rather than judging yourself for feeling emotions, allowing them to motivate you to be open to the best experiences possible for your life.

4. If there are still painful memories haunting your present life from earlier times, be willing to complete these memories by calling back whatever energy you dispersed in those relationships and situations using recapitulation (see *Chapter Six*).

3. Working with Your Subconscious Mind

Your subconscious mind can be your biggest tool for positive change. Memories are stored in the subconscious. The subconscious is like a little five-year-old child who responds well to rewards. To work with your subconscious, it is often helpful to get into brain wave states other than beta. You can do this by:

1. Creating a daily meditation practice.

2. Engaging in a Qigong and/or Yoga practice.

3. Committing to bodywork sessions with skilled practitioners who understand the power of allowing "the body to remember what the mind forgets" (Joseph Moreno) to bring up suppressed emotions stored in the body.

4. Working with effective hypnosis and/or guided meditation audio programs.

4. Transforming Beliefs

As I stated earlier, beliefs are connected to your emotional responses and can be transformed when you work with your conscious and subconscious mind. Some of the ways to reach the subconscious mind are to install affirmations while you are in an altered state of mind that encompasses being out of the beta brain wave state and into the alpha or theta brain wave states (see *Chapter Four* for details).

These altered states can be reached through meditation, repetition (for example chanting, or repeating specific mantras), and self-hypnosis and guided meditations. Beliefs are connected to your emotional responses. Beliefs can be transformed when you work with your subconscious mind through altered states, repetition, meditation, hypnosis, and guided meditations.

5. Support Systems

There are various types of support systems, including Mastermind groups (see, e.g., *www.thesuccessalliance.com*), Twelve Step groups, online and in-person support systems connected with courses (such as B.E.S.T.), church and community groups, etc. Search online, ask at your local library, or contact my organization accessed through the website: wwwterrywohl.com. I recommend establishing a consistent support buddy from your friends or contacts at one of the aforementioned groups is highly recommended.

Keep in mind that these support systems will only be effective if you keep your goals current and in your daily thoughts, words, and actions. Utilize these various support groups to provide you with a way to be 'accountable' for your commitments. For instance, I have a Women's Wisdom Circle that meets three times a week on the phone. Each week, I ask the group to "hold for me", to visualize for me the successful completion of each goal for the week. To be more specific, I may ask the group to hold for me the completion of a specific chapter to be accomplished within one to three weeks, depending on the length and complexity of the material.

6. An Evolutionary Journey versus a Final Destination

Rather than think of your journey as having only one final destination, it is helpful to think of your evolutionary process as a journey that contains many wonderful destinations along the way. For instance, if you were taking a yearlong trip around the world, you would not just be focused on one destination. Instead you would be open to discovering new cultures and sights at each stop along the way.

Studies have shown that the people who tend to keep choosing stimulating activities tend to live the longest and have the healthiest minds.

Ongoing learning of new information and skills will keep your brain active and vital. We live in a world that is rich with information and opportunities to expand your skills and knowledge. It is also a proven fact that the stimulation provided by continued learning will help your brain stay healthy and possibly even help your brain build reserves of new brain cells. *("Live a Long Life"* #8 WikiHow *www.wikihow.com/Live-a-Long-Life*).

7. Physical Activity

Physical activity will help you to increase your energy levels by increasing your oxygen intake and blood flow. We have already addressed the activities of moving meditations, yoga, and Qi Gong. It is also good to emphasize the value of aerobic activity. Dance classes, step classes, and running activities (that are done in a way that protects your joints) are all types of helpful exercises.

8. 21 Days (or fewer) to Reinforce New Habits

According to many doctors, coaches, authors and neurobiologists, it takes twenty-one days to form and strengthen new neural pathways in the brain [Maltz, *Psycho-Cybernetics*, p.xiii). So when you want to change a particular habit, practice the new way of doing it for twenty-one days. When you maintain a new practice for at least twenty-one days, it becomes an established habit within your neural pathways.

9. Continuing Your Progress

- Review all the outcomes of your homework assignments. Decide which ones you want to continue to practice throughout in the next twelve months.

- Practice each stress management technique for twenty-one days until it becomes an automatic habit.

- Keep your Present View (PV) to Best View (BV) of your future images in a visible place to see every day. Post your PV to BV and say to yourself: PV to BV ten times a day.

- Connect with your support structure on a daily basis.

Additional Ways of Boosting Your Confidence/Making Progress:

- Read spiritual material that inspires you.

- Connect to a relevant Internet support group.

- Take the 150-Day Challenge of meditating on a Psalm a Day.

- Journal the positive developments in your life, because "Energy Flows Where Attention Goes".

- Clear out your mind clutter and the clutter of your home and workspaces.

- Write out the details of what your *ideal day* would look like and feel like. For instance, what time would you be getting up in the morning and what would you be doing with your day and evening.

- **Tracker for Your Goals:** Set up a Year-Long Tracking Document where you record your Goal for the Year and your success in accomplishing the steps to achieving your yearlong goal and perhaps your ten-year plan goals.

- **Month:** Set up a document where you record your monthly progress.

- **Week:** Set up a document where you record your weekly progress.

- **Day:** Set up a document where you record your daily progress.

- Find a daily goal buddy with whom you can check in via 15-minute phone conversations or Email communications. During these communications, note what you have accomplished, what you still need to do. Notice if anything is blocking the accomplishment. Talk about this with your goal buddy, and brainstorm together ways to move through the blocks. Also, note your conversations, so you can observe where you began, where you are, and where you are going.

- Utilize Post-It Notes to help you keep track of your daily commitments.

- **Post illustrations around your home that inspire you:** Find images that inspire your subconscious mind. Perhaps you can create a vision board, where you take compelling images of the things you want to experience in life. Make a collage of these images and display it in an area of your home where you are bound to see it every day.

- Keep the Filters Chart within reach so you can check what filters you are utilizing in your language and communication patterns (see *Chapter Two*).

- Create your own Audio Self-Hypnosis file.

- Create story forms about your current life and the life you aspire to live.

- Study the Drama Triangle formation (see *Chapter Five*) and create a more empowering new position for yourself – such as standing above, below, in the center, or to the side of it. Most importantly, keep breathing through your emotions related to each Drama Triangle position and create a new internal and external dialogue regarding each position.

- Think of your present position in life as an opportunity to be a Fork in the Path – where you are in possession of the Master Control Switch. Do this with your thoughts and your actions.

- **Track Switching:** When you realize you are thinking negative disempowering thoughts, change tracks and choose more empowering thoughts. This can also use this technique to help the people in your life who are experiencing trauma. When these people are in an agitated disempowered state, acknowledge their emotions (so they feel heard and understood) and then say empowering things to them. This will also settle into both your subconscious mind and their subconscious minds, because when people are in an overwhelming emotional upset, they are usually acting out of their younger (child) selves that is innately connected to their subconscious mind. If you realize that this upset is an opportunity for you to directly access their subconscious mind as well as your own subconscious mind, you can experience powerful evolutionary benefits and results.

10. A Blessing for Your Journey

May you always breathe into your value and loveliness, affirming that God has graced you with life and this world with you.

May your Divine Light and Presence
always be a blessing to you and our world.

Thank you for taking this journey with me. May you carry whatever goodness you have experienced by doing this work into all realms where it will be graciously appreciated and received.

There is only one you, so remember that as you make your way through this world, God has gifted life to you and gifted you to this world. So it is. Blessings Be Ever Yours.

Terry Anne

Works Cited

A

Allen, Lynne. *Our Life is How We Speak It: The Impact of Our Words.*

Amen, Daniel G., MD. and David E. Smith, MD. *Unchain Your Brain 10 Steps to breaking the addictions that steal your life.* California, Amen Clinics Inc., MindWorks Press. 2010.

August, Jenn. *Remove Your Blocks So Your Business Rocks.* PDF file from website: *www.beyond-business-for-women.com.* 2009.

B

Bandler, Richard. *Get The Life You Want: The Secrets to Quick and Lasting Life Change with Neuero-Lingusitic Programming.* Deerfield Beach, Florida: Health Communications, Inc., 2008

Bandler, Richard, John Grinder. *Frogs Into Princes Neuro Linguistic Programming.* Moab, Utah: Real People Press. 1979.

Brunelle, Beverly, Terry Wohl. Akashic Record and Channeling Prayer. *www.BeverlyBrunelle.com* and *www.TerryWohl.com.* 2011.

C

Cameron-Bandler, Leslie. And Michael LeBeau. *The Emotional Hostage, Rescuing Your Emotional Life.* Moab, Utah: Real People Press. 1968.

D

Dayton, Tian Ph.D. *Emotional Sobriety.* Deerfield Beach, Florida: Health Communications, Inc. 2007.

Dayton, Tian Ph.D. *The Living Stage, a Step by Step Guide to Psychodrama, Sociometry and Experiential Group Therapy.* Deerfield Beach, Florida: Health Communications, Inc. 2005.

Dayton, Tian Ph.D. *Trauma and Addiction Ending the Cycle of Pain Through Emotional Literacy.* Deerfield Beach, Florida: Health Communications, Inc. 2000.

Dayton, Tian Ph.D. *Emotional literacy resolution model (Trauma and Addiction).*

Dayton, Tian Ph.D. *Neuroscience and Psychodrama: Validating the Mind/Body Approach of Psychodrama.* www.asgpp.org/html/article1.html 2011.

Desikachar, T.K.V. *The Heart of Yoga: Developing A Personal Practice.* Rochester, Vermont: Inner Traditions International. 1995.

Dilts, Robert with Tim Hallbom, Suzi Smith. *Beliefs: Pathways to Health & Well-Being.* Portland, Oregon: Metamorphous Press.1990.

Dilts, Robert. *The Article of the Month Modeling the Wisdom of Jesus.* NLP University (www.nlpu.com/Articles/artic27.htm) 1996. Web. 12 Sept. 2010.

Du Preez, *Leadership Consultancy* (www.executivecoachasia.com).

Du Preez, Quote found in: Google Answers.

G

Gordon, David. *Therapeutic Metaphors: Helping Others Through the Looking Glass*. Cupertino, California: Meta Publications.1978.

H

Hedva, Beth Ph.D. *Betrayal, Trust, and Forgiveness: A Guide to Emotional Healing and Self-Renewal*. Berkeley, California: Celestial Arts.1992.

K

Kingsland, James. Age-Old Story. 23 January 1999 Number 117 *New Scientist* 13/10/2001 Updated 24/7/2002 *members.fortunecity.com/templarser/geront1.html*.

L

Levine, Peter A. Ph.D. *Healing Trauma, A Pioneering Program For Restoring Wisdom Of Your Body*. Boulder, Colorado: Sounds True, Inc..2005.

Levine, Peter A. Ph.D with Ann Frederick. *Waking The Tiger Healing Trauma*. Berkeley, California: North Atlantic Books. 1997.

N

Navarro, Joe with Marvin Karlins, Ph.D. *What Every Body Is Saying*. 10 East 53rd Street, New York, NY 10022 Special Markets Department, Harper Collins Publisher. 2008.

R

Rosenblum, Lawrence. *See What I'm Saying: The Extraordinary Powers of Our Five Senses*. New York, New York. W.W. Norton & Company, Inc. 2010.

S

Smart, Jamie. *The Hidden Power of Meaning: The Top 10 Tips for Reframing & Belief Change with NLP* www.saladltd.co.uk 2008.

Sri Siva. *The One Minute Guide to Prosperity and Enlightenment.* Oakmont, Pennsyvania: Vaak Sounds. 2002.

W

Wolinksy, Stephan Ph.D. *The Way of the Human. The Quantum Psychology Notebooks Volume II. The False Core and the False Self.* Capitola, California. Quantum Institute. 1999.

Internet Sites

www.thetaobums.com/index.php?/topic/13629-tongueroof-of-mouth.

How to Do the Cobra Breathing Exercise - eHow.com www.ehow.com/how_2322034_do-cobra-breathing-exercise.html#ixzz0w8xEoji7.

ads.associatedcontent.com/www/delivery/ck.php?n=a14de4a 9&cb=931981424.

www.nlpu.com/Articles/artic27.htm.

wiki.answers.com/Q/What_is_Greek_meaning_of_the_word_ believe.

www.youramazingbrain.org/lovesex/sciencelove.htm.

www.fiftyisthenewforty.net.

Microcosmic Orbit. Boston Healing Tao. Marie Favorito, Director. Web. www.bostonhealingtao.com/ microcosmicorbit.php. 12 Aug. 2010.

Zhang, Sloppy. *Tongue/Roof of mouth* The Tao Bums Discussions On the Way. Web. 22 Sep. 2008.

www.thetaobums.com/index.php?/topic/13629-tongueroof-of-mouth 12 Aug. 2010.

Reninger, Eliazbeth (Whisper). *The Inner Smile: A Meditation Practice.* Associated Content from Yahoo Health and Welness. 29 June 2006. *ads.associatedcontent.com/www/delivery/ck.php?n=a14de4a9&cb=931981424* 12 Aug. 2010.

Dir. Richard Vagg. Narr. Erick Thompson. *The Brain* Darlow Smithson Productions. History Channel. 2008. DVD.

Pick, Marcelle. OB/BYN NP. "Deep breathing — the truly essential exercise." Women to Women *www.womentowomen.com/fatigueandstress/deepbreathing.aspx.* 2/16/10. Web. 8/10/10.

en.wikipedia.org/wiki/Belief.

www.merriam-webster.com.

Your Amazing Brain..." The Science of Love. *www.youramazingbrain.org/lovesex/sciencelove.htm.*

Fat Free Yoga - Lose Weight & Feel Great for Beginners & Beyond w/ Ana Brett & Ravi Singh. *www.raviana.com/aboutravi.html.*

Google Answers Q: Feelings and Emotions (Answered) *answers.google.com/answers/main?cmd=threadview&id=149261*

Allen, Lynne. *Our Life is How We Speak It: The Impact of Our Words.* *www.selfgrowth.com/articles/our_life_is_how_we_speak_it_the_impact_of_our_words.html.*

An Examination of Obama's Use of Hidden Hypnosis Techniques in his Speeches. *www.internet-grocer.net/hypnosis.pdf.*

Hintz-Zambrono, Katie Style in the News *www.stylelist.com/blog/2009/10/06/katy-perry-interviews-karl-lagerfeld-elle.com*.

Master Hypnotist - Caught on Tape, Get Drunk without Beer at: *www.youtube.com/watch?v=gdDNcuBeD3I*.

Olmstead, Edward, *Intentional Focusing Meditation Exercise*. *www.youtube.com/watch?v=NcKP5_Bo9D*.

Definitions of Beliefs *www.merriam-webster.com/dictionary/beliefs*.

Definitions of Transformation: *www.merriam-webster.com/dictionary/transformation*.

Kingsland, James. Age-Old Story. 23 January 1999 Number 117 *New Scientist* 13/10/2001 Updated 24/7/2002 *members.fortunecity.com/templarser/geront1.html*.

August, Jenn. *Remove Your Blocks, So Your Business Rocks*. beyondbusinessforwomen.com © 2009 Beyond Business, LLC.

Brunelle, Beverly. *www.beverlybrunelle.com* 2011.

Czach, Dave. *Einstein Method to Rapid Solutions*. 2003. *www.ofspirit.com/daveczach1.htm*.

About the Author

Terry Anne Wohl's commitment is to support people in reconnecting with their Divine Cores and in developing and maintaining their Divine Connections in all aspects of their lives.

Terry Anne Wohl is a certified: Mind-Body Vibrancy Coach, Shiatsu and Thai Yoga Practitioner, Hypnotherapist. She holds a Doctorate in Divinity from the American Institute of Holistic Theology.

Terry is a keynote speaker, a workshop leader, and tele-seminar facilitator.

Her extensive research since 1984 has afforded her the great honor to study, assist, and teach with some of the top leaders in the human potential industry such as Kam Yuen, Margot Anand, and Ethel Lombardi.

Terry has also studied with Gay and Katie Hendricks, Larry Crane, Stephen Wolinsky, Vernon Wolfe, Chuck Duff, and Ohashi.

Terry is a contributing writer for whole life publications such as The Aspectarian and Unity Magazine.

She is an accomplished painter and has exhibited her work at the Aspen Art Museum and in galleries in Philadelphia and Chicago.

She can be contacted at
TerryWohl@hotmail.com
For more information about Terry's courses, lectures, and related work go to: www.terrywohl.com.

www.ingramcontent.com/pod-product-compliance
Lightning Source LLC
Chambersburg PA
CBHW070755100426
42742CB00012B/2146